D0955191

CLEAN+DIRTY DRINKING

CLEAN+DIRTY
DRINKING

100+ Recipes for Making Delicious Elixirs, With or Without Booze

GABRIELLA MLYNARCZYK

PHOTOGRAPHS BY GRANT CORNETT

CHRONICLE BOOKS
SAN FRANCISCO

Library of Congress Cataloging-in-Publication Data

Names: Mlynarczyk, Gabriella, author. | Cornett, Grant,
    photographer.
Title: Clean + dirty drinking / by Gabriella Mlynarczyk ;
    photographs by Grant Cornett.
Other titles: Clean and dirty drinking
Description: San Francisco : Chronicle Books, [2018] |
    Includes bibliographical references and index.
Identifiers: LCCN 2017025825 | ISBN 9781452163819
    (hc : alk. paper)
Subjects: LCSH: Cocktails. | Alcoholic beverages. |
    LCGFT: Cookbooks.
Classification: LCC TX951 .M59 2018 | DDC 641.87/4—dc23
    LC record available at https://lccn.loc.gov/2017025825

Manufactured in China

Food and prop styling by Maggie Ruggiero
Designed by Alice Chau
Typesetting by DC Typography

10 9 8 7 6 5 4 3 2 1

Chronicle books and gifts are available at special quantity
discounts to corporations, professional associations, literacy
programs, and other organizations. For details and discount
information, please contact our premiums department at
corporatesales@chroniclebooks.com or at 1-800-759-0190.

Chronicle Books LLC
680 Second Street
San Francisco, California 94107
www.chroniclebooks.com

For Iggy, I raise a glass to you, wherever you may be!

INTRODUCTION

To drink or not to drink? That is the question!

Is it nobler to treat your body like a temple, imbibing only that which makes you stronger? Or to live fast, die young, and leave a legend of debauchery on the journey to meet your maker? I've walked both paths and, along the way, I found my balance. Too much of *anything* and you'll find yourself in trouble; as Buddhist teachings tell us, we will find peace in the middle ground.

A PLEASURE TO TASTE

Don't get me wrong—I'm not a born-again bartender, and I'm not going to spout Vedic scripture or suggest a week of standing on your head to negate the weekend's indulgent practices. As a trip through this book will show you, I believe that feeding both your body and your soul doesn't have to be as unfulfilling as that plate of alfalfa sprouts and mashed yeast that Woody Allen turned his nose up at in *Annie Hall*. My philosophy is this: If a drink is going to pass your lips, even if the emphasis is on its health claims, it should be a pleasure to taste. And if, on the contrary, it's a boozy bev, it could and should be beneficial in some way—after all, most spirits were invented for medicinal purposes, even while they came with the (often addictive) side effect of making imbibers feel high.

I came to bartending in 1986. Back then, I had champagne taste on a tap water budget, but as a lover of fashion and a student of the "rag trade," I felt it was my duty to be decked out in what my peers and I considered the best. Bartending filled my pockets with just enough money to keep my closet full of vintage cool and my lips painted with Chanel lipstick. Bartending was a job; it was never supposed to be a lifelong commitment. And yet, somehow, over time, it got into my blood.

That said, from my longtime position behind the bar I've had the opportunity to watch some badass chefs in their element and soak up some of their tricks. When I step up to that slab of wood, my shy, oddball, inner kid transforms into a Martini-stirring diva with confidence for days. Although some of my 9-to-5-er friends criticize me for not having a "real" job, bartending has given me a flexible lifestyle: I can pack up and come and go as I please, and meet someone new every single day. And it's a creative outlet as well, feeding my artistic hunger to constantly reinvent—if not myself, then at least what is in the glass before me. It's also the reason I get to write this book!

A CONNECTION TO THE EARTH

I come from a family of culinary tinkerers, inventors-by-necessity, and experimentation artists. My Pops Iggy was a musician and the master of both the Newkie Brown hot toddy (a blend of Newcastle Brown Ale warmed and blended with honey and, sometimes, garlic) and the perfect cup of tea. My mum and my aunts Janine and Judy were always on a mission to one-up each other with the lightest pastry recipe. Gramps was a gifted gardener: I swear, if he planted a toenail, he could grow a human. My witch-doctor Gran could banish "demons" from your head with a spirit-wrapped tea towel and a fireside chant, and she also taught me the discipline of working with needles: embroidery, crochet, and invisible hems. She drilled into my head at an early age the folkloric maxim, "If you don't have good thoughts in your mind, what you have in your hand will come to no good." And she was right!

My unorthodox family, a clan of foreign outsiders in suburban England, was very Catholic, but at the same time paganish, you could say, in our connection to the earth we stood on and the seasons that governed our diet. My summers were spent digging for earthworms or lounging under sunflowers eating a bucketful of bush blackberries. Seasonality was not a choice; it was how my grandparents ate. And, so in turn, seasonality inspires my drinks: each is an ode to the time of year or a fresh ingredient at its growing peak.

Another big influence on my cocktail styling is that from my home-growing roots to my DIY adulthood, I never had much of a budget for luxuries, such as pricey mixers and other extras. So, as a bartender, and out of necessity, I adapted my recipes to whatever ingredients I could forage: fresh seasonal fruits and vegetables and herbs, or year-round oils, vinegars, teas, and dried herbs and spices. This practice earned me the moniker the "Pantry Raider" at Ink restaurant, where I worked for a spell for genius chef Michael Voltaggio.

MODERN BARTENDING

But I'm getting ahead of myself. As I waded into the world of watering holes, I picked up some training while working in London for Terence Conran, where my first "mixed drink" was a white wine spritzer requested by R&B goddess Sade. Later, in New York, an Earl Grey Tea Sour whipped up by Audrey Saunders of Pegu Club changed my life forever. The perfection of this drink sang to me—and my brain worked overtime to figure out how it was made. Around the same time, I was introduced to two exceptionally skilled bartenders well versed in pre-Prohibition-style cocktail making. I had simply never tasted drinks so good, and I owe my fledgling cocktail education to them—thanks, Audrey, for providing that initial spark, and Lynnette and Jim for filling in the numerous gaps!

A few years later, after several hundred incredibly hazy nights and several hundred more beautifully made cocktails, I found myself relocating to Los Angeles for a reset. L.A.—the land of eternal sunshine, where the abundance of the seasonal harvest made me feel like the proverbial kid in the candy store. This was produce like I'd never seen before, piled high in farmers' market stalls: fragrant Thai basil blossoms begging to be sniffed; fat, bulging Japanese tomatoes; melt-in-your-mouth Seascape strawberries winking bright red and tasting like Mother Nature had intended. I felt like it was my ordained duty to celebrate this phenomenal edible bounty.

Modern bartending is so much more than just throwing ice in a shaker, pouring in some booze, waving the shaker about, and tossing it all into a glass with a radioactive cherry. Some of my colleagues could rightly be called chefs due to their commitment to craft, attention to detail, and perfectionism. A good bartender spends hours prepping for service before the doors open. We make fresh juice, prepare syrups and infusions, carve ice, and cut or fine-tune garnishes, as well as polish glasses, stock wines, beers, and spirits, and tidy up from the night before. Let's say service lasts five hours, or as much as seven or eight; then another hour or two are dedicated to cleaning up and breaking down. All told, it's a time-consuming and arduous job . . . but addictive. For me, each drink is an opportunity to make a better version than the last. I love the adrenaline rush, the fast pace, working as part of a team, and connecting with my guests, many of whom have, over the years, become my friends. My other cherished "friends" are my tools; we work as a team and without them I would be nothing.

MY BOOK: YOUR CREATIVITY

Chapter One of this book presents the vital information you need to understand, or reconsider, all the steps to creating a delightful beverage, beginning with the basics—the tools, your *mise*. From there I move through the mechanics of foundational techniques, such as measuring and stirring, but including things like how to make a simple (or complex) syrup, which ice to use and when, and how—and how many times—to shake a drink.

Chapter Two explores the wide vista of all the wonderful things you could (and should) choose—forage— for making an exceptional drink, from syrup and juices to usual and unusual items from the market and the pantry selected based on a philosophy of using fresh and potent (in terms of flavor or health benefits—or both) ingredients, from freshly squeezed citrus juice to modern foams, all with a cherry on top—or rather, a lovely updated garnish, such as a Parmesan Frico (page 137).

Chapter Three contains the recipes, organized by season. Every drink has a booze-free (Clean) and a liquor-laced (Dirty) version. "Clean" drinks are any cocktails that are nonalcoholic and that, for the most part, do not contain processed sweeteners, using instead more beneficial sweeteners, such as raw honey, maple syrup, or coconut nectar—all of which contain an abundance of amino acids beneficial to our bodies.

I created a Clean and Dirty version of each drink for a couple of reasons. I no longer enjoy that hungover feeling from too much sugar or alcohol, and my ability to function and recover after drinking sugary or boozy cocktails has diminished exponentially as I've gotten older. I didn't want to be that boring old fart drinking soda water but, rather, preferred to join the festivities with tasty, fun drinks. (I don't think I'm alone here.)

It's up to you, the drink maker—and the drink drinker—to decide which version you prefer on any given day. Get creative. Yes, this is my book and these are my guidelines, but I'm writing it for you to pick up, devour, color outside the lines, and create your own combinations. The possibilities are unlimited.

To your health!

CHAPTER ONE:
MISE

My journey as a bartender began in a pub with the most basic information: recipe + presentation, or the "Knowledge," as we liked to call it. I wasn't making anything more complicated than a Martini or an Old-Fashioned, but the details mattered, nonetheless, when endeavoring to make a good drink and get customers to come back for more. Without the correct measurements, the drink would be too weak or too strong; without knowing whether to shake or stir, the ingredients would not be properly combined; without a clean presentation, you would be serving a drink with no sex appeal. The chef I am working with as I write, Brendan Collins, a fellow Brit, likes to say, "Make it sexy"—regardless of whether he's talking about executing delivery of a cocktail, cleaning up a spill on a plate, or tidying the worktable. Taking his cue, when I talk about making it sexy, I mean making a drink so beautiful that heads turn in a room.

Making the perfect drink requires learning everything from how to whip the fluffiest aquafaba (or egg white) to which basic shaking motion works for your style of drink. Much of my job is not glamorous—encumbered with tedious tasks like seeding lemons or clearing a clogged drain—but these moments keep it real and also keep it transcendent, giving me time to think and conjure my next libation.

Mise en place, or "mise," is a French term that translates to "putting in place" or "everything in its place." And, in this case, I use it specifically to refer to putting in place your basic wares, tools, ingredients, and accoutrements—the things that suit you and your creations and that will help you build a better cocktail—the things you need and want at the ready in your creative space. So, let's dive into the basics to establish our foundation before moving forward into all levels of the cocktail arts.

TOOLS

Just like all cooks and chefs, a bartender or drink maker should start with a clean, organized workspace equipped with efficient tools of the trade. A roomy countertop and access to a sink come first and foremost. And while many techniques can be improvised, there is nothing more crucial—and pleasurable—for producing the results you want than a good-quality, reliable tool designed for the task at hand. See page 124 for a separate rundown on tools especially useful for creating garnishes.

BASIC YET
HARDWORKING TOOLS

Most bartenders have their favorite tools and will tote their tool roll to every job. That kit usually contains some or all of the following: measuring spoons and long-handled bar spoons, jiggers, paring knives, peelers, muddlers, reamers, strainers, and shaker tins. These trusted helpers make our jobs easier and make us more efficient. My personal collection also includes a well-sharpened chef's knife (and a portable knife sharpener to keep it that way), kitchen scissors, a lighter for flaming citrus peels, small tongs for handling garnishes, an iSi whip and chargers, an immersion circulator for sous vide preparations (see page 67), resealable plastic bags, and a digital scale.

The following list includes some of my favorite basic yet hardworking tools plus a specialty item or two. Some are for your kit, some are less portable. It can get you started and help you adapt as your skills and interests grow. You may not (yet! . . . I can't live without mine) see the need for an immersion circulator, for example—although if you love the idea of a quick route to homemade bitters, you may come around to it—but you might love strainers of every kind, from standing to handheld in every degree of mesh to full-on

decorative showpieces, and want to collect them all. It's a personal thing. In addition, of course, you will need a few cutting boards, large and small sharp knives, and a constant supply of clean kitchen towels.

BLENDER

Regular models serve nobly for many functions in the blending realm, but for the power and versatility needed for more ambitious projects, investing in a heavy-duty blender opens a lot of doors.

USED FOR blending, grinding, puréeing

I LOVE Vitamix Vita-Prep

CARBONATOR

Contains a chamber for liquids and a lid with a carbonation system either built in or attached; CO_2 is pumped through the lid into the chamber to change still liquids into sparkling ones.

USED FOR making fizzy cocktails and soft drinks

I LOVE Perlini Carbonated Cocktail System

CHINOIS STRAINER

Deep, conical strainers with more surface area than the usual bowl-shaped sieves and extra-fine mesh for rendering liquid mixtures super silky and smooth; some come with stands so you can let them filter slowly and/or wooden pestles to help you push the mixture through.

USED FOR straining infusions, juices, etc.

I LOVE Matfer Exoglass bouillon strainer

COCKTAIL SHAKER (OR SHAKER TIN)— A.K.A. THE BOSTON SHAKER

Two stainless steel cups or tins—a small and a large one—that cocktails are built and shaken in.

USED FOR shaking drinks

I LOVE Koriko weighted tin set

COCKTAIL STRAINERS

Small stainless steel specialty strainers designed to fit on top of a shaker tin or mixing glass to strain out ice as well as things such as muddled herbs and fruits when you decant the liquid into the serving glass. There is a range—some have holes that intentionally let through bits of fruit or little shards of ice, others are meant to deliver a pristine elixir. Standards include Hawthorne, Julep, and other simple versions, such as small, fine-mesh conical styles.

The **Hawthorne strainer** is a stainless steel paddle-type shape with tightly wound coils attached to it. The coils trap errant particles such as leaves or ice shards. The **Julep strainer** is akin to a slotted spoon only with a shorter handle and is used to strain stirred cocktails. The holes allow the liquid to pass through whilst the spoon shape catches the ice. The **CoCo strainer** is a smaller version of the mesh chinois cap strainer used in the kitchen, also similar to a tea strainer. It has a small cone of fine stainless steel wire mesh attached to a handle. It is used in conjunction with a Hawthorne strainer to finely strain or double strain a cocktail.

USED FOR straining drinks

I LOVE Koriko Hawthorne, Cocktail Kingdom Julep, Cocktail Kingdom CoCo

IMMERSION BLENDER

Two-part blending gadget with a motor set into a handle connected to the blades at the other end; insert it into pitchers and pots of mixes to blend, purée, or make foams.

USED FOR blending or frothing liquids

I LOVE Cuisinart Smart Stick

IMMERSION CIRCULATOR

Long box-like contraption that encases a heating coil, a motor, and temperature controls; insert it into water baths to heat the water and keep it a consistent temperature.

USED FOR rapid infusing, barrel aging, sous vide preparation

I LOVE PolyScience Creative series

JIGGERS

Small stainless steel measuring cups with notches marked inside to denote various liquid amounts. Standard sizes include ½ fl oz, ¾ fl oz, 1 fl oz, and 1½ fl oz [15 ml, 22 ml, 30 ml, and 45 ml].

USED FOR precisely measuring small amounts of liquid

I LOVE Leopold vintage reproductions, Japanese style (solid, steeper-angled walls, multiple measures etched inside), or the simple Danesco multilevel jigger

JUICER (CITRUS)

A reamer with a spout on top of a spinning motor.

USED FOR juicing citrus and pomegranates

I LOVE Waring Pro

JUICER (VEGETABLE)

A mechanical screw-like press attached to a slowly turning motor that pulverizes veggies and fruits. Because there is no rapidly spinning blade, there is no kinetic friction or heat buildup to destroy essential vitamins in the produce.

USED FOR juicing all manner of fruits and veggies

I LOVE SKG wide chute model

MANDOLINE

Handheld slicer with a variety of interchangeable blades set into a plank of wood, plastic, or stainless steel.

USED FOR creating very thin, uniform slices of fruits and vegetables

I LOVE Japanese-style Benriner

MICROPLANE

Related methinks to a woodworker's rasp (a coarse metal tool with ridges used for filing wood or, sometimes, metal); the Mircroplane has a metal shaft with mini grater blades that, when rubbed against citrus or nutmeg, for instance, shaves off small pieces.

USED FOR mostly garnishing and finishing drinks such as egg nog, whipped drinks with foam or cream, etc.; finely grating fruit zests and nutmeg, citrus peel, and chocolate

I LOVE Microplane 40020

MIXING GLASS

Large glass pitcher without a handle, although some larger old-school models have handles to make picking them up easier; insulated stainless steel is my preference of late because the metal conducts temperature and distributes it to chill cocktails faster.

USED FOR stirring clear drinks

I LOVE Cocktail Kingdom 25 fl oz [750 ml] stemmed mixing glass

MIXING (OR BAR) SPOONS

Sturdy, long-handled stainless steel spoons, usually about 12 in [30.5 cm] long.

USED FOR stirring drinks, especially in pitchers and tall glasses; cracking ice

I LOVE Cocktail Kingdom Teardrop; less expensive versions can be found online

MORTAR AND PESTLE

Bowl (the mortar) with a spout paired with a blunt club-like object (the pestle) most often made out of wood or marble; a rudimentary grinding machine traditionally used for preparing medicine, herbs, and food.

USED FOR pounding herbs, spices, and coarse salt

I LOVE Milton Brook 5.25 in [13 cm] ceramic, HIC marble

MUDDLER

Club-like stick, usually 9 to 12 in [23 to 30.5 cm] long. Similar to the pestle (listed previously), made from wood or sometimes food-grade plastic, it has either a textured or smooth end used to mash ingredients. It also serves as a weapon when you have an unruly customer at your bar . . . another story, perhaps? . . .

USED FOR muddling (lightly bruising) ingredients such as citrus wedges or fresh herbs to bring out the flavorful oils

I LOVE OXO, Cocktail Kingdom "Bad Ass" muddler, or the OXO stainless steel version

MULTIPURPOSE WHIP

Stainless steel canister with a gas charger (uses CO_2 and NO_2 gases) attached at the top.

USED FOR whipping cream, creating foams, carbonating

I LOVE iSi Culinary Gourmet Whip

PEELER

Very sharp blade similar to a vegetable peeler but set into a catapult-shaped handle that makes it easier to hold and control when stripping off peel for garnish. Watch that your fingers don't get in the way; it may take the tops off if you're not careful.

USED FOR removing citrus peel twists or larger strips of zest, shaving ice corners

I LOVE OXO Good Grips Y peeler

SPICE GRINDER

Similar to a coffee mill, with a blade set on top of a motor, a cup that holds the ingredient to be ground, and a lid to stop it from flying everywhere.

USED FOR grinding fresh whole spices into a fine powder

I LOVE Krups F203

TWEEZERS

Pair of metal sticks fused at one end, similar to cosmetic tweezers, and used for precise placement of ingredients.

USED FOR handling garnishes, picking out unwanted bits from drinks before presentation

I LOVE Fluval Flora planting tongs, Mercer Culinary precision tongs

GLASSWARE

Just as important to consider as garnish and ice is glassware—scents and bubbles need to be properly presented or their effect evaporates or is lost. For instance, a highly aromatic drink should be served in a glass that traps those wisps of scent. A "Scaffa," a mixed cocktail comprising all clear spirits, served without chill or dilution at room temperature, similar to a brandy or cognac, should be served in a snifter-type glass so the heat from your hand as you hold the glass encourages the cocktail's aromas to develop. A cocktail finished with a spritz of citrus oil is best served in a stemmed coupe-style glass (think: vintage champagne glass) or wineglass that best preserves that scent. A spritz is best in a wineglass so the bubbles are trapped inside the glass and hit your nose as you drink. A Julep should be served in a metal cup so the metal's conductivity helps retain the chill longer for this summertime classic. Following is a selection of glasses I use often behind the bar. I look for vintage or unusual modern versions for my collection. Vintage coupes can be picked up in Goodwill stores for pennies.

Since many drinks I make are based on a narrative, I also like to use unconventional "vessels" for serving them. A brown rice–based Mai Tai with Chinese five-spice powder is offered in a Chinese take-out box, or my riff on a frozen Daiquiri using garden herbs is served in a small terrarium. My point? Why stick to plain old glasses when you can have some fun with your drink's appearance and create a talking point for the business. The quirky presentations become an instant social-media marketing tool.

GLASS TYPES

Coupe glass

Legend has it that the coupe, a saucer-like glass set on top of a stem, was molded after Marie-Antoinette's left breast. From its creation, it was originally used as a champagne saucer for special occasions, but as fashions in champagne changed, so, too, did the glass. With the classic cocktail revival the coupe was resurrected as an old-school alternative to the commonly used Martini glass.

USED FOR Manhattan cocktail and its variations, Martinis, East Sides, sours (both pisco and whiskey)

Double Old-Fashioned glass or rocks glass

A short, squat glass used traditionally for serving brown spirits and cocktails, such as the Old-Fashioned. The base is usually thicker and the glass has a wide mouth, so ingredients can be muddled inside it.

USED FOR Old-Fashioned cocktails, Sazerac, smashes such as the Whiskey Smash and Gordon's Cup, and sour cocktails such as a Margarita and the Penicillin

Collins glass/highball glass

A tall, cylindrical tumbler, its name comes from the Tom Collins cocktail usually served in it. In addition, a selection of mixed drinks, both alcoholic and nonalcoholic, are served in it.

USED FOR Tom Collins, John Collins, fizzes such as the Ramos Fizz, beer cocktails such as the Michelada, Mojitos, Bucks, and Mules

Snifter

A type of stemware for aged brown spirits that includes a large balloon-shaped glass with a fat bottom and a narrower mouth. The large surface area allows the spirit to evaporate. The aromas are trapped by the narrower mouth so when it is lifted to the mouth to drink, the nose fits inside and breathes in the scents. The glass is also sometimes used with beers that have a higher ABV (percent of alcohol by volume). The correct way to hold the glass is to cup the bottom of the balloon in your palm; the stem should rest between two of your fingers. I use a stemless snifter for many of my drinks—both Clean and Dirty (the drinks, not the glass!)—because they are often finished with an aromatic spritz. I like to call this glass the goldfish bowl.

USED FOR Serving single pours of brandy, cognac, Armagnac, Calvados, Scaffa cocktails, and beers such as stout, porter, and IPA

Wineglass

Similar in design to a snifter, the wineglass is generally a balloon with a narrow opening set upon a longer stem than the snifter. Again, the wine's aromas are trapped inside the glass so they can be inhaled as the wine is drunk. There are many shape varieties but, in general, the mouth of the glass should never be wider than the bottom. A more fragile wine, such as a red burgundy or Pinot Noir, is best served in a bigger balloon so its delicate aromas have more surface area to evaporate from whilst being trapped by the narrower opening. Smaller versions are used for sherry and other liqueurs. The correct way to hold a wineglass, especially when drinking cold wine, is to grasp it by the stem. Holding it by the balloon part of the glass warms the wine too quickly.

USED FOR Wine, sparkling wine, spritzers, and punches

TECHNIQUES

More than anything else, making a perfect drink takes focus and the ability to follow a recipe to a T. But that focus must be combined with the right tools and well-constructed, accurate recipes. Simple as it may seem, mixing drinks is science, governed by precise measurement. Just as in baking, if you don't adhere to the formula, your dough will never rise, or your cookies will be hard as hockey pucks, and winging it when mixing drinks will result in an unbalanced waste of liquid that never gets the chance to sing.

What follows are the basic techniques of drink making, in the general order of the actual process, starting with an understanding of how to build flavor. Ice comes second (though it comes into play at different points, it needs to be ready). Next is the drink's construction—from selecting the correct glass and measuring ingredients to muddling, stirring, shaking, or otherwise "cooking," and ending with straining. Garnishing is last, of course, but because it's such a both broad and nuanced subject, with so much magic, it has its very own section.

BUILDING FLAVOR

In my time as a decadent, pleasure-seeking woman, I sampled many a bartender's drinks. Sometimes, I admit, I was a total snob, and sent back glasses in which the balance was off—too much alcohol, too sweet, too sour, too wet and watery. But I think that's fair. Sad to say, but a lot of bartenders get into this industry for the cool factor. They learn all sorts of tricks for tossing their shakers around, winking at the ladies or gents, reveling in their moment as "star-tenders" on stage, without studying the basics. Of course, part of our job is to entertain and keep guests coming back; some well-known bar gurus have even said they would endure crap drinks if they loved their bartender. But I'm demanding. I want a whore behind the bar keeping me entertained and an angel whipping up perfection in a glass for me.

What some bartenders forget (or forgo) is that the perfect drink should have a balance among sweet, sour, aromatic, and bitter; fingers of aroma should entice you to the glass. The first sip should begin with a punch of flavor that gradually evolves as it travels across your tongue, with a lasting finish and not too much burn from the spirit—just like a fine wine.

My basic formula for a generally well-balanced drink is as follows.

THE FLAVOR TEMPLATE

- ¼ cup [60 ml] **clean or spirit base** (which can be broken down into two or three ingredients as long as they equal ¼ cup [60 ml])
- 2 Tbsp [30 ml] **sweet**
- 2 Tbsp [30 ml] **sour**
- ¾ tsp **bitter**
- ¼ tsp **smoked salt**
- ¾ tsp **pure vanilla extract** (an optional addition to soften a cocktail)
- **Garnish** for aroma

You can divide the base and the sweet and sour amounts among two, or even three, ingredients—for example, a base of 1 fl oz [30 ml] each of gin and sherry, or equal parts simple syrup and a liqueur for the 1 fl oz [30 ml] of sweet. The bit of bitters adds balance and finish, and, believe it or not, that bit of salt makes a huge difference. The aromatic garnish can be anything from a charred pepper to a small nosegay of mint or geranium, a spritz of citrus oil, etc.

This is just one example from a master formula I have found that ensures balance. Not all drinks follow this straightforward formula; some veer onto a very different path to find their bliss. You can reduce or increase the sweet and sour elements, for example.

If you take that path and reduce or increase a sweet element, you need to balance the drink by either reducing or increasing the sour element, too (or your drink will be lopsided), and the amount of your clean or spirit base. Feel free to experiment, but keep this formula in mind.

MOUTHFEEL

While calibrating your components, also think about mouthfeel—a slightly inscrutable term that tries to capture other sensual elements of a perfect bite or sip. For your cocktail: Do you want it light and bubbly and, thus, requiring a sparkling element, such as soda, beer, or champagne? Or do you want it unctuous and smooth, a texture you can achieve by fat-washing (see page 105), adding a protein emulsifier, such as aquafaba or egg white (see page 118), or shaking in a viscous gum syrup (see page 73)?

IT'S NOT ALL ABOUT THE BASE

As you learn and explore how to balance flavors in the perfect cocktail, never forget: It's not all about the base. I consider a well-made drink—whether a pint of beer, a glass of wine, or a cocktail—to be similar in construction to mélanges, from stews to perfumes: an array of top, middle, and base notes that change as they warm on the tongue, in the belly, or on the skin. Whether drinking or eating or smelling, the flavors should happily develop and transform. Our taste buds are, essentially, thousands of minute sensory organs, and each

area in the mouth picks up a different flavor quality.

I think of top notes as being the most aromatic, those you encounter as your mouth and nose sidle up to the rim of your glass—a spritz of grapefruit oil, a hint of smoke, a touch of jasmine or bergamot. The middle note is the sweet, sour, or savory component of the drink. It may be the botanicals in gin or mezcal; the vanilla in a barrel-aged spirit, such as brandy, Calvados, rum, or whiskey; or the spices in an infused syrup. Finally, the base is how the drink ends. Crisp and mineral? Smoky, spicy, or bitter? The right garnish, even as simple as a mint leaf or citrus twist, also plays a part in this flavor symphony. Often, garnishes seem in the way and are discarded to lie neglected and unloved on a beverage napkin. Next time, consciously focus on the garnish while you taste your drink and let it do its thing; you may notice a big difference in how each sip goes from beginning to end.

There is a vast palette to work with when mixing drinks, from simple syrups to juices and consommés to nut milks to shrubs and homemade bitters. The Heroes, Superpowers + Sidekicks lists (see page 41) provide an at-a-glance reference for ideas to build flavors, but can also inspire you to explore new territory.

THE RIGHT ICE

Ice Ice Baby! Often just as overlooked or underestimated as it is rendered in beautiful neoclassical forms: Ice—that crucial building block you may be tempted to treat like water—is key in the world of mixed drinks. Jeffrey Morgenthaler, bartender god, said it best when he quipped, "Ice is to the bartender as fire is to the chef." Paradoxically, though, ice can also be the enemy—think: dilution. The role of ice is indeed similar to fire; it "cooks" the drink as it brings everything together. But too much ice in your drink just makes a glass of watery rubbish. So control your desire to fill your shaker with a giant scoop of ice—it can wash most of the flavor away.

SHAPED ICE

Ice: It's not just for cubes anymore. At work I don't have a budget for ice, and it doesn't cost much to equip yourself with the right ice at home, either. While I do depend on my commercial Kold-Draft icemaker, we also use inexpensive silicone molds, available in tons of shapes and sizes online and in kitchen-supply stores, to create a fun variety of ice. For fancy events, I get a giant ice block and have my way with it, carving it into smaller blocks with a bread knife. Hand-hewn cubes are beautiful, crystal clear, and look stunning in your glass.

Following, though, are a few of my must-haves for ice.

Kold-Draft ice cubes and refrigerator ice

These are used for shaking or filling a glass. The Kold-Draft ice makes perfect 1-in [2.5-cm] -square cubes; because Kold-Draft ice machines are mostly available in commercial sizes, I suggest the silicone trays that produce a cube similar to Kold-Draft's. If making your own small cubes is not for you, by all means use standard freezer ice cubes—just remember that the flake- and crescent-shaped cubes your freezer dispenses melt far more quickly due to their thinner shapes and break into pieces as you shake, so work quickly to avoid dilution.

When using Kold-Draft ice for whip shaking (see page 35), I crack the ice into a couple of smaller pieces and use one or two of them to give my drink a slight chill without too much dilution; the more of those small pieces used, the faster dilution happens. Kold-Draft ice and refrigerator ice are not the best ice to use for shots of expensive spirits; for those, read on.

Both types are the workhorse ice of cocktail making, good for most drinks served on the rocks—from water to mixed drinks, such as Margaritas or Negronis.

Rock cubes and spears

Rock cubes are those cubes about 2 in [5 cm] square you see at many a savvy bar—happily becoming more common in drinks (usually more simple pours) served on the rocks. Unlike crushed ice or regular cubes, the bigger cubes keep the drink cold while they melt very slowly, guaranteeing a really good cold and tasty drink all the way down to the last drop. One rock cube fits perfectly into a double Old-Fashioned glass (see page 20).

There is also a long ice cube called a spear that is used in highball-style (Collins) glasses (see page 21) for the same purpose. The mold is often sold as a "Collins mold."

Also good in Margaritas, Negronis, and Old-Fashioneds, spears are great in tall drinks such as gin and tonics and—yes—Tom Collinses.

Spherical ice (my favorite)

This is a large, glamorous orb (I guess that means we can't call it a cube). The shape is optimal for slow, consistent melting that delays dilution; even with big rocks cubes, the corners melt off more quickly. And a sphere is a thing of beauty! Spherical ice is typically about 2.5 in [6 cm] in diameter and fits into double Old-Fashioneds as well as stemless wineglasses—for the latter, I love those big glasses shaped like fishbowls because, like a brandy snifter, they trap aroma inside the glass.

If you decide you really like round ice, there's a nifty tool called the ice ball maker. They are pricey, ranging from $160 to $800, but they make a sphere—*presto chango*—like magic—out of a small block mold. My local Japanese market also sells ice balls. Overall, spherical ice is not for the economy minded, but if you want to impress someone, they're worth tracking down. Avoid those silicone spherical ice molds; they take too much time and effort to perfect, and, so far, I have not had much success using them.

These are good in almost any spirit you want a chill on but with minimal dilution, such as expensive whisky or other high-end spirits.

Pebble (pellet) or nugget ice

Fill a serving glass with this ice. It looks exactly as it sounds, like little pellets or pebbles, and it melts really fast because of its small size. It's for any swizzled drink, such as the Caribbean and tiki classics. These drinks are mostly built in the glasses they are served in and so get no dilution from shaking. The spirit will be hotter or stronger because of this and pebble or pellet ice gives you the necessary amount of dilution to make the cocktail crushable. Don't mistake pebble ice for crushed ice, which is far too fine and should be reserved for shaved ice syrups and cooling food or storing garnishes.

For cracking ice, if I can't get my hands on pebble ice, I use the standard wider bar spoon with the red knob on the end. They're cheap, they're cheerful, and they're only really good for this one job (as well as maybe stirring big pots of syrup or mixers). It's not as consistent in shape but, in a pinch, it does the trick.

Pebble ice is good for boozy Julep- and Mojito-style drinks or sweeter cocktails that can withstand some rapid dilution.

BDX silicone cocktail cube

In addition to "real" ice, there is the silicone cube. When added to a drink, the motion of shaking it with such a large cube (about 2 in [5 cm]) creates bubbles and adds oxygen to the drink, which opens up the structure of the ingredients. This non-ice substitute was created by master inventor/ chef, Dave Arnold, both to save the expense of going through a lot of big rock cubes and to provide more control over dilution; it can be found on the Booker and Dax website and from other bar tool sources.

These are great for aerating a drink and adding to the texture of the finished cocktail.

FLAVORED ICE

Another way of adding complexity or interest to a drink is with flavored ice. It can be as simple as freezing cucumber juice into ice cubes for a glass of sparkling water, or making a frozen stock cube that gradually adds its "seasoning" to the drink as it dissolves. Following are two of my favorites for flavored ice—a cool clean watermelon agua fresca and an instant Old-Fashioned—just add booze. But use either recipe and the lists beginning on page 42 to invent your own combinations.

OLD-FASHIONED STOCK ICE CUBES

MAKES 18 STOCK ICE CUBES

With flavored versions of big, beautiful rock ice cubes, you have an enticing drink that practically makes itself. I call these "stock ice cubes," and make them in many varieties to keep in the freezer.

In the following recipe, which creates beautiful cubes studded with tartness and color and scented with honey, plus a touch of bitters—it's all there!—I would add whisky or mezcal. (Bonus: The reishi tincture includes immune-boosting and liver-detoxing properties.)

18 orange zest strips, about 1 in [2.5 cm] long and 1 in [2.5 cm] wide (from 1 or 2 oranges)

18 Drunken Cherries (page 131)

18 dropperfuls reishi tincture

2 cups [480 ml] Miso–Manuka Honey Syrup (page 70)

4 cups [960 ml] filtered water

¼ cup [180 ml] amaro bitters, preferably Cynar or Fernet Francisco

Clear a level space in your freezer to fit a small, rimmed baking sheet. Place three silicone rock ice-cube trays, each with six compartments about 2 in [5 cm] square, on the sheet for stability (silicone trays are wobbly and you don't want to lose precious liquid in transit).

In each mold compartment, put 1 piece of orange peel, 1 Drunken Cherry, and 1 dropperful of reishi tincture. Set aside.

In a pitcher, stir together the syrup, water, and bitters. Pour the mixture into the molds, filling each compartment about three-fourths full. (The volume expands as the liquid freezes and this makes for a neater cube.) Carefully transfer the sheet

to the freezer and freeze for at least 8 hours, until completely solid.

To release the ice cubes, remove from the freezer and let sit at room temperature for about 5 minutes (less if you're in a hot room), just until the cubes start to pull away from the sides of the molds. Turn the molds upside down over a large bowl and carefully peel the sides away from the ice cubes until they drop into the bowl. Keep frozen in an airtight container or resealable plastic for up to 1 week.

"MAKES ITSELF" COCKTAIL

1 Old-Fashioned Stock Ice Cube

¼ cup [60 ml] liquor of choice

Add the stock cube to a double Old-Fashioned glass. Pour the liquor over and enjoy. If you're in a particularly indulgent mood, keep topping up your glass until the stock cube vanishes.

WATERMELON, MINT + BASIL ROCK ICE CUBES

MAKES 18 LARGE ROCK ICE CUBES OR 2 TRAYS OF MINI ICE CUBES

The mini cubes are used in cocktail #7 (page 171) for a summery Julep; the larger version can be used in a variety of drinks, including a glass of sparkling water, a wine spritzer, or a vodka and soda.

4 cups [600 g] cubed watermelon
10 sprigs fresh mint
5 sprigs fresh basil
2 cups [480 ml] filtered water

Clear a level space in your freezer to fit a small, rimmed baking sheet. Place three silicone rock ice-cube trays, each with six compartments about 2 in [5 cm] square, on the sheet for stability (silicone trays are wobbly and you don't want to lose precious liquid in transit).

In a juicer, process the watermelon, mint, and basil. You can also use a blender, but the juicer results in far more liquid. Pour the juice through a chinois or other fine-mesh strainer into a large bowl or pitcher. Add the water and stir to combine.

Pour the mixture into the molds, filling each compartment about three-fourths full for the large cubes (the volume expands as the liquid freezes and this makes for a neater cube), or fully for the mini cubes, which visually suffer less for being a bit wonky. Carefully transfer the sheet to the freezer and freeze for at least 8 hours, until completely solid.

To release the ice cubes, remove from the freezer and let sit at room temperature for about 5 minutes (less if you're in a hot room), just until the cubes start to pull away from the sides of the molds. Turn the molds upside down over a large bowl and carefully peel the sides away from the ice cubes until they drop into the bowl. Keep frozen in an airtight container or resealable plastic bag for up to 1 week.

MEASURING

Winging a drink by haphazardly pouring arbitrary amounts of liquid into a glass does not make for a successful or tasty cocktail. As in baking, exact measurements are crucial to the success of a drink's balance: add too much brown sugar to your cookie batter and you end up with a pool of goo on your baking sheet; add too much citrus juice to a cocktail and you will have wasted time, effort, and product by creating an undrinkable mixture. Take time to measure your ingredients correctly. There are no shortcuts when mixing drinks.

That said, the correct tool for measuring ingredients for drinks is a mini-measuring cup called a jigger. Standard jiggers are two-sided, with a different measure on each end and an hourglass shape that makes them easy to grip for a steady pour. Essential sizes are a 1-fl oz [30-ml] + 2-fl oz [60-ml] jigger and a ½-fl oz [15-ml] + ¾-fl oz [22-ml] jigger. There are many variations in style, shape, and material, of course; my absolute favorite

to look at is called a Leopold jigger. It has a second set of measurement lines marked inside so you don't have to switch jiggers—providing a number of options at your fingertips. I'm also fond of the Japanese jigger, again for its aesthetics, and it fits nicely between my fingers. Its extra-tall, steep sides make accurate measuring even easier. The jigger I use most for speed behind the bar is an inexpensive multilevel jigger from Danesco because I don't need to waste time flipping it over or switch it out for a smaller size. It's not fancy to look at but, like me, it is a workhorse behind the bar.

When measuring a partial pour in your jigger, such as a ½ fl oz [15 ml], fill the jigger exactly to the desired line; when using a full measure, for example 2 fl oz [60 ml], carefully pour to the very top of the 2-fl oz [60-ml] jigger so the liquid comes to a convex fill at the jigger's edge. This is called a meniscus.

MUDDLING

Muddle, muddle, toil, and trouble! Personally, I'm just not a huge fan of the muddled drink—texturally, it just doesn't work for me. I'm not really into chewy bits in my straw or drinks—unless, I guess, it's a smoothie. Even then I blend the mix heartily. Muddling, a kind of gentle crushing done with a long wooden or rubber-headed steel pestle is, admittedly, a fast way of imparting flavor to the drink. The problem with muddling, to me, though, is that, especially with delicate herbs, such as mint, you are very likely to end up with a muddy-tasting drink rather than something full and bright. The aim is to gently press the flavorful oils out of the herb's leaves without destroying them completely; I let the ice in my shaker do the bashing instead. It delivers just enough force to break up the leaves and release the flavors. I do use muddling for tougher ingredients, such as cucumbers, kumquats, or chile peppers.

The muddler I favor is the Badass muddler made from food-grade plastic, or an OXO stainless steel muddler with a nylon head, for a few reasons: Wood is porous and soaks up flavor over time, so I don't feel I get totally clean flavor with a wooden muddler. I also find these easier to keep clean, and they fit nicely in my hand.

Muddling itself is a fairly simple process. Put ingredients in the bottom of your cocktail shaker or mixing glass. Using gentle downward pressure with your muddler, press into the ingredients, moving the muddler's head around so each piece gets even attention. If you decide to defy me and muddle your herbs, make sure you strip them from the stems and muddle only the leaves; stems can release woody or earthy flavors into the mix. Vibrant aroma and flavor is all you're after.

To strain a muddled drink, I employ two strainers stacked together—a Hawthorne strainer and a CoCo strainer—to trap even the smallest of inevitable bits created during muddling (see Straining, page 37).

STIRRING/MIXING

"Cooking" a cocktail (see The Right Ice, page 25) involves stirring/mixing, and also shaking/whipping (see page 35) to properly mix a drink, along with that most valuable of ingredients, ice. Without either, you have a jumble of ingredients sitting in a glass. While some of you may argue it all goes down the same hole, it takes a bit more finessing to make a cocktail come to life and turn it into a pleasurable experience. To better understand which approach to take, read on. . . .

Stir it up, little darlin'! To shake or to stir? The answer is actually quite straightforward: Any clear drink that contains no juice is stirred in a mixing glass with ice. That gives the best chill with minimum dilution and produces a thoroughly blended mixture of (hopefully) pristine clarity. The whole point of a stirred clear cocktail is to taste some of that heat from the spirit. Shaking a clear drink will over-aerate it, resulting in an unappealing cloudy appearance, and it washes out that heat so you don't taste all its nuances. Sometimes a guest at my bar wants a shaken Martini—I will, of course, oblige, as it is my job to provide a guest what she orders. But, to be honest, I think a stirred Martini is the way to go. Shaking results in little chips of ice that dilute the Martini too much and create a watery cocktail as opposed to an unctuous, smooth one.

The tool for this process is called, aptly enough, a mixing spoon, or bar spoon—essentially a long-handled, very sturdy spoon. A mixing spoon must have a good weight, but should not feel clunky. It's also important that it have a twisted handle to give you a better grip, and that ergonomically it feels comfortable for your height and hand size. For stirring drinks, by far my favorite tool is the simple weighted spoon with a teardrop end from Cocktail Kingdom. I use the 12-in [30.5-cm] spoon with a twisted handle that twirls nicely in my hand.

STIR

Stirring a drink is an acquired skill: You need to practice. Hold the spoon between your thumb and first finger and roll the twisted handle between them as you stir your drink. This action gives you the maximum amount of molecular agitation and contact with the ice. Following are my standard ways of stirring a cocktail—always add ice last.

Stirring Method for Cocktails Served UP in a Coupe- or Martini-Style Glass without Ice

Build the drink in a chilled mixing glass (see page 34) starting with the least expensive ingredients, such as bitters and simple syrup, and finishing with the most expensive. That way if you make a mistake you do not waste precious ingredients.

Add 5 or 6 Kold-Draft, or similar, ice cubes and stir for 10 to 15 seconds. This allows enough time to chill the drink without it becoming overly watery and, because it won't be diluted further by being served on ice, you should stir a little longer than cocktails served down (method following). Also I should mention, do not rest your hand on the side of the mixing glass. The heat from your hand slows the chilling process. You want your mixing glass to remain as cold as possible. Strain the drink into your chilled glass to serve.

Stirring Method for Cocktails Served DOWN in a Double Old-Fashioned, or Similar, Glass with Ice

Build the drink directly in a chilled glass (method following), again starting with the least expensive ingredients.

Add 4 or 5 Kold-Draft, or similar, ice cubes and stir 5 or 6 times. This short stir gives enough chill to the cocktail without eliminating the spirit's heat. It also means that as the drink dilutes it should only change in flavor slightly as the ice melts; stirring for too long results in a cocktail that is good only for the first few sips, after which it becomes too watery.

SWIZZLE

Another stirring method is called *swizzling*, for which you need a bar tool called a swizzle stick. This is not that little plastic thing in your Piña Colada; a barkeep's swizzle stick is a long stick with prongs at the end, either a narrow fork with several tines or 4 or 5 prongs in a sort of star for-mation. Swizzle sticks are necessary for stirred drinks built in a glass with lots of ice, such as Juleps. They are especially useful for any drinks that have smaller pieces, such as mint and sugar, in the bottom.

Swizzle It, Just a Little Bit

To swizzle a drink, thrust the swizzle stick into the ice and spin it between your palms like you're making fire with sticks. The little prongs on the end whirl the contents of the glass together. Dilution is not so much a worry here—a swizzled cocktail is perfect for summer. It's usually tall and cooling and, as the ice melts, also a great hydrator on a sticky hot day.

I'm not a huge fan of the tool that combines a spoon on one end and a swizzler on the other. The metal surface does not provide enough traction or give me enough of a swiz-zle. And when using the spoon end, I find the swizzle end uncomfortable to hold.

***

CHILL!

Because fridge space behind a bar is generally prime real estate and very limited, and while you may have room for a glass or two at home—but not a whole party's worth—I offer here my quick tip for properly chilling glasses.

To chill a glass quickly, I add 3 or 4 ice cubes and fill the glass with soda water. The salt in the soda water supposedly helps make the ice colder. Do this 1 to 2 minutes before you need the glass to build the drink in, just make sure to empty it com-pletely before adding your cocktail ingredients.

SHAKING/WHIPPING

The standard cocktail shaker, also called a shaker tin, is actually a pair of tins, one smaller [typically 18 fl oz, or 530 ml] and one larger [28 fl oz, or 840 ml] that fit together at the open ends. They should be weighted so they don't tip over while you build drinks in them, and they should be easy to press on to release the seal once the drink is shaken. My preferred style is made by Koriko. (Note: NEVER use a pint glass with a shaker tin for shaking—it's just plain dangerous, especially when trying to crack open the two parts of your shaker. The glass can easily shatter onto you, onto your customers, and into your ice.)

There is also a classic small shaker that comes in three pieces: the tin, the built-in strainer, and the cap. This is called a cobbler shaker. It's smaller than the standard cocktail shaker, holding about 17 fl oz [500 ml] maximum. If you choose this shaker style, you will most certainly need a CoCo strainer to finely strain your drinks because the holes in the strainer portion of the cobbler shaker are large enough to allow shards of ice and bits of herbs, such as mint, to pass through.

When building a shaken drink, I generally work in the small shaker because its lower sides help me see what's inside. Add the ingredients, follow with the ice, and place the large shaker on top. I tap the upper tin with the heel of my hand to make a sturdy seal. Flip the assembly over so the smaller shaker is always on top. The reason: If the seal breaks, the shaker's contents won't end up all over me and the guest in front of me. After shaking, separate the tins by pinching the top of the larger one into an oval, breaking the sealed connection.

The smaller the ice you use, the less time you need to shake. Shake times also vary depending on the drink you're making. For example, if the drink is served on teeny-tiny pellet ice or pebble ice, don't shake too long or you'll have a watery drink. A drink served up, such as a Cosmopolitan, can be shaken longer because the drink will not be under attack from dilution in the glass and you want it chilled all the way down. Here's a rough guideline:

WHOLE LOTTA (OVER) SHAKING GOING ON

Drink Served	Shake Ice	Shake Time	Shake Style
Up	6 cubes	10 seconds	Hard shake
On a large rock	5 cubes	7 seconds	Hard shake
On Kold-Draft, or similar, ice cubes	4 cubes	5 seconds	Hard shake
On pebble ice	1 cube	3 seconds	Whip shake

The hard shake is the one employed by most classic cocktail-making bartenders and is used for the majority of shaken drinks served on larger ice cubes, such as Kold-Draft or a rock cube. The ice in the tin rapidly travels from the shaker's end to end combined with as high a velocity as possible. When I train new bartenders, I tell them to imagine they're throwing a rugby ball across the field (in the United States you could imagine a baseball). You want this kind of strength behind it; just don't let go—you may break a window, or worse!

The whip shake is a lot gentler. It's used to either aerate an emulsifier, such as egg whites or, in my case, aquafaba (see page 118), or to blend ingredients well and add just a slight chill. I also use the whip shake for shaking drinks served on pellet, or pebble, ice. The action is achieved by adding 1 or 2 small ice cube pieces to the shaker and employing the same kind of movement as the hard shake with half the thrust behind it.

The dry shake is used similarly for emulsifying ingredients, such as aquafaba or egg whites (see page 118). I stopped using this method because, all too often, my shaking tins would crack open with their contents thrown all over my shoulder. The reason they crack open is that you are adding air to the emulsifier, which puffs up their strands. The increased air has nowhere to go, so it pushes the tins apart—kind of like a mini bomb that releases energy from the inside. I always use the whip shake instead because the small amount of ice chills the shaking tins just enough to contract them together and form a firm seal (remember your science classes?).

One special note about shaking drinks: I often use a polyethylene "cocktail cube" (see page 27) to bring more air and texture to both emulsifiers and my shaken cocktails. Shaking emulsified drinks with one large "ice" cube somehow makes the drink "fluffier." The action of that large cube being tossed around in the liquid creates more small air bubbles, which hold for longer—again, the magic of science. To get the same kind of aerated texture without it, you need many more real ice cubes in your shaker tins, which create too much dilution. For shaking a cocktail, I use the fake ice cube for its weight and a couple of Kold-Draft ice cubes for chill and dilution.

STRAINING

The strainer's job is to separate the cocktail from the ice and any other ingredients mixed with the liquid, such as mint or cucumber, for flavor but not for serving. For shaken drinks, the Hawthorne strainer is the only one for me; for straining, I love the Koriko brand. Its tightly wound springs allow only liquid through—no ice chips, no mint leaves. It also fits nicely in my hand and the handle is the perfect length. I find many strainers have overly long handles, which get in my way. The Koriko Hawthorne strainer also works on stirred drinks and fits neatly into my mixing glasses; other makes of Hawthorne strainers are too small to fit onto most mixing glasses.

The classic strainer for stirred drinks is called a Julep strainer. It looks like a slotted spoon with an abbreviated handle. Cocktail Kingdom has a good selection.

Sometimes, if I'm without my trusty Koriko, I will double strain a drink to make sure it is clear: I fit a Hawthorne strainer over my shaker and then place a CoCo strainer underneath that, to catch errant ice chips or flotsam. When straining, place the strainer over the shaker and push the coils against the inside; they will trap everything but the liquid in your tin.

THE ESSENTIAL BAR

I'm often asked what the ideal home bar should look like. The answer, of course, depends very much on your drinking habits. Mine are limited these days, but I still love an after-dinner digestif or a drop of whisky after a tortuous shift at work. I also lean toward the lower-ABV selections, such as vermouth, sake, and sherry, to round out my essential bar's needs. In any case, many of us love variety or want to have anything a guest may desire (within reason) on hand. Following are my suggestions for thoughtfully produced bottles for making a huge range of drinks, in the base (spirit), mixer, and bitters categories.

SPIRIT

APERITIF
- St. George Bruto Americano
- Cocchi Americano
- Contratto

BRANDY, CALVADOS, COGNAC
- Germain-Robin
- Le Compte
- Park

DIGESTIF
- Cynar
- CioCiaro
- Nardini
- Varnelli Amaro Dell'Erborista

GIN, DRY
- Peak Spirits
- Ford's
- Botanist

GIN, OLD TOM
- Hayman's
- Ransom

MEZCAL
- La Niña
- Del Maguey
- El Jolgorio

RUM, DARK
- Santa Teresa
- Hamilton
- Diplomatico

RUM, LIGHT
- Rum Society
- Rhum JM
- Clement

SAKE
- Sakura
- Akashi

SHERRY
- Alexander Jules
- Alvear
- Lustau

TEQUILA

- Agua Riva
- Siete Leguas
- Don Camillo

VERMOUTH

- Ransom
- Dolin
- Alessio

VODKA

- Peak Spirits
- Black Cow
- Bainbridge

WHISKEY, BOURBON

- W. L. Weller
- Hudson
- Old Forester

WHISKEY, JAPANESE

- Yamazaki
- Nikka
- Chichibu

WHISKEY, RYE

- Rittenhouse
- Few
- Willet

WHISKY, SCOTCH, BLENDED

- Compass Box
- Ballantine's
- Bank Note

WHISKY, SCOTCH, SINGLE MALT

- Springbank
- Auchentoshan
- Ardbeg

MIXER

- Chartreuse
- Contratto
- Curaçao, dry
- Falernum
- Giffard
- Maraschino
- Pimento Dram

BITTERS

- Angostura
- Cardamom
- Celery
- Chocolate
- Firewater tincture
- Orange
- Peychaud's

HEROES, SUPERPOWERS + SIDEKICKS

Over time I've come to realize that the path to a less-guilt-ridden life is to make sure that anytime I put something into my body—cocktail or food—it should include an ingredient that will somehow offer me a health benefit. For instance, why have a glass of refreshing (but sugary) lemonade when you can make it taste just as delightful by swapping out the processed sugar for something less refined (think: raw honey, maple syrup, coconut nectar) that still contains essential minerals? Or to add extra flavor, juice some kale, turmeric, or ginger and add that to your glass. And if, on occasion, I want to add a shot of gin or mezcal, at least the goodness in that beverage can balance some of the negative side effects of getting your buzz on with the old firewater. For example, turmeric, a powerful inflammatory, can help lessen that hangover pain and ginger will put the kibosh on the queasies.

To make a perfect drink, you have to learn the various components. Why use lime juice instead of lemon juice? How do I add a layer of background flavor? Why shake instead of stir? In this section and with detailed lists, I present a condensed core curriculum to help with the main questions about the "mix" in mixed drinks.

My drinks always start with what I call the "hero" ingredient—anything from apples to oolong. I choose these core ingredients, and call them by that name, because of their beneficence. Not only do they contain nutritional prowess (their superpowers) that lends them greatness, but they also have wonderful, deep, complex flavors that put standout characteristics at the center of a delicious drink—like the hero character stands out in a story.

And then, of course, there's the spirit. Note, though, that while the alcohol in my drink recipes is as carefully chosen for balance as all the other factors, many of my drinks start as "fauxtails," without the liquor. I then add the spirit in increments to the hero base; that way, it never competes or bullies out the delicate flavors of strawberry or basil, for example. As in perfume blending, I consider my top, middle, and base notes to achieve a perfect balance of flavors (see page 23). And also, if you approach it that way, it makes the following lists, with their guidance in choosing healthy ingredients for drinks that also have tons of potential for building great flavor, work just as well for clean drinking.

The mix now requires an acid, almost always citrus juice for shaken drinks—the acid is essential to balance any sweeter elements. Just as sugar is needed to enhance flavors, citrus juice works to brighten a cocktail and stop it from getting too cloyingly sweet. Other acids I use are vinegars, shrubs (see page 108), and malic acid, a natural powdered derivative that contributes to the sour taste in apples and grapes. It also has various health benefits, including preventing bacteria in the mouth and boosting energy.

Finally, the trusty sidekicks, or accents, are incorporated to complement and build on the hero's strengths.

Hero ingredients have become an essential part of my daily life, so I take any chance I can to get my dose, which is how they wound their way into my cocktails; after all, if you're going to have anything pass your lips, it should somehow make a positive contribution in your body and your path to longevity. If you get into the habit of adding a hero or two into your daily diet, they will more than balance out your decadent fixes (when moderation doesn't work). I see it as osmosis at work.

Start with this list of hero ingredients. For each, superpower capabilities—such as anti-inflammatory or digestive aid—are listed, as well as the best sidekicks to make them shine even more. Think of this as a list of culinary equations to make a better-tasting drink: Hero + Spirit + Citrus (acid) + Sidekick. For every hero, you can shuffle out the options for components as you like (for example, apples have a choice of twelve sidekicks and eleven spirits; other heroes have a short list of compatible citrus, as well). If you stick to the ratio detailed in Building Flavor (see page 23), you'll be creating your own recipes in no time.

APPLE

SUPERPOWER Antioxidant, cancer fighting, allergy tamer, cholesterol reducer

SPIRIT Aged rum, amaro, aquavit, bianco vermouth, bourbon, calvados, dry sake, dry vermouth, gin, tawny port, vodka

CITRUS Lemon

SIDEKICK Allspice, beet, caramel, caraway, cardamom, Chinese five-spice powder, cumin, fennel, ginger, smoked salt, wood smoke

AVOCADO

SUPERPOWER Cholesterol reducer; high in vitamins C, E, K, and B; high in fiber; loaded with potassium

SPIRIT Cachaça, dry sake, falernum, Manzanilla sherry, mezcal, vodka, yellow chartreuse

CITRUS Lemon, lime

SIDEKICK Allspice, chocolate, cilantro, pepper, pineapple, togarashi

BLACK SESAME

SUPERPOWER Rich in vitamin B, calcium, iron, and antiaging chemicals; keeps bones strong; cancer and cholesterol fighter

SPIRIT Aged rum, amaretto, amaro, bourbon, Calvados, dry sake, scotch, tawny port, vodka

CITRUS Lemon

SIDEKICK Cinnamon, ginger, honey, maple syrup, nut milk, smoked salt, tahini, vanilla

BROWN RICE

SUPERPOWER Reduces insulin spikes, high in fiber, fights cholesterol

SPIRIT Aged rum, aged sweet sherry, bourbon, mezcal, nigori sake, scotch, tequila

CITRUS Lemon, lime

SIDEKICK Anise, cardamom, Chinese five-spice powder, cinnamon, honey, kaffir lime leaf, maple syrup, orange flower water, orange liqueur, pineapple, raisins, vanilla

CARROT

SUPERPOWER Powerful cancer fighter; antioxidant agent; high in vitamins A, K, C, and B_8

SPIRIT Aperol, aquavit, Bianco vermouth, dry sake, dry vermouth, gin, mezcal, vodka, white port, yellow chartreuse

CITRUS Lemon, yuzu

SIDEKICK Cardamom, coconut, cumin, fennel, ginger, parsley

CHAMOMILE

SUPERPOWER Antibacterial, fights diabetes, calms nervous system, promotes healthy skin

SPIRIT Aquavit, Bianco vermouth, dry sake, gin, Grüner Veltliner, Riesling, scotch, vodka

CITRUS Lemon, yuzu

SIDEKICK Bee pollen, cardamom, coriander, goat's milk, green tea, honey, lavender, orange flower water, royal jelly

COCONUT

SUPERPOWER Excellent immune booster, antiviral, antibacterial, great source of fiber, loaded with vitamins and minerals, helps prevent osteoporosis

SPIRIT Amaro, cachaça, falernum, gin, mezcal, pisco, rum (all), sake (all), scotch, tequila, vermouth (all), vodka

CITRUS Lemon, lime, orange, yuzu

SIDEKICK Allspice, chai tea, galangal, ginger, holy basil, kaffir lime leaf, lemongrass, matcha green tea, mint, pineapple, Thai basil, turmeric, vanilla

CRANBERRY

SUPERPOWER Phytonutrient rich, anti-inflammatory, cancer fighter, high in vitamin C

SPIRIT Aquavit, Bénédictine, Campari, dry sake, genepy, gin, kümmel, Manzanilla sherry, red wine, rye, vermouth (all), vodka, white port

CITRUS Lemon, lime, orange, yuzu

SIDEKICK Allspice, anise, Chinese five-spice powder, cumin, genepy, ginger, orange flower water, orange liqueur, thyme

ENGLISH PEAS

SUPERPOWER Antiaging, blood sugar regulator, high in vitamins A and C and omega-3s

SPIRIT Bianco vermouth, dry sake, dry vermouth, gin, vodka, white burgundy, white port, white rum

CITRUS Lemon, yuzu

SIDEKICK Carrot, coriander, cumin, mint, nasturtium, smoked salt, sumac, tarragon, thyme

FENNEL

SUPERPOWER Antioxidant agent, immune support, high in vitamin C and potassium

SPIRIT Dry sherry, gin, kümmel, orange liqueur, red wine (all), ruby port, sake (all), vermouth (all), vodka, white port, white wine (all)

CITRUS Lemon, lime

SIDEKICK Allspice, apple, blood orange, celery, coriander, cumin, ginger, grapefruit, orange, orange flower water

GRAPEFRUIT

SUPERPOWER High in vitamin C, blood pressure tamer, stabilizes blood lipid levels

SPIRIT Amaro, brandy, dry sake, dry sherry, gin, kümmel, mezcal, pisco, ruby port, rum (all), tequila, vodka, whisky (all), white port

CITRUS Lemon, lime, orange, yuzu

SIDEKICK Allspice, bay leaf, black pepper, Chinese five-spice powder, cinnamon, coriander, cumin, fennel pollen, fennel seed, orange flower water, pink peppercorn, sumac

GUAVA

SUPERPOWER Helps control inflammation, helps prevent oxidative stress, high in lycopene and vitamin C

SPIRIT Chartreuse, cachaça, Drambuie, gin, pisco, port, rum (all), scotch, sherry, tequila, vermouth (all), vodka

CITRUS Lemon, lime, yuzu

SIDEKICK Allspice, cardamom, cinnamon, coriander, ginger, honey, orange flower water, smoked salt

KUMQUAT

SUPERPOWER Phytochemical rich, high in vitamins A, C, and E; antioxidant agent

SPIRIT Aquavit, brandy, dry sake, dry sherry, kümmel, pisco, ruby port, rum (all), scotch, vodka, white port

CITRUS Lemon, lime, yuzu

SIDEKICK Allspice, bay leaf, black pepper, Chinese five-spice powder, coriander, cranberry, cumin, fennel pollen, fennel seed, orange flower water, pink peppercorn, sumac

LEMON VERBENA

SUPERPOWER Anticandida boosts immune system, protects muscles from stress, soothes nerves

SPIRIT Cherry liqueur, genepy, gin, orange liqueur, pisco, ruby port, sake (all), vermouth (all), vodka, white port, white rum, wine (all), yellow chartreuse

CITRUS Lemon, orange, yuzu

SIDEKICK Almond, black cherry, green tea, smoked hay, tonic water, vanilla, white tea

LETTUCE

SUPERPOWER Aphrodisiac badass; high in vitamins A and C, and calcium; rich in omega-3s

SPIRIT Bianco vermouth, chartreuse, dry sake, dry vermouth, Floc de Gascogne, gin, sauvignon blanc, vodka, white port

CITRUS Lemon, yuzu

SIDEKICK Black pepper, celery, celery seed, coriander, cucumber, fennel seed, lemon thyme, smoked salt, sumac, tarragon

MISO

SUPERPOWER High in amino acid–rich protein, detoxifier, free-radical fighter

SPIRIT Dry sake, dry sherry, dry vermouth, dry white wine, mezcal, rye, scotch, vodka

CITRUS Lemon, lime, orange, yuzu

SIDEKICK Bay leaf, black pepper, celery, honey, maple syrup, mushroom, rosemary, sage, smoked salt, truffle, wood smoke

NASTURTIUM

SUPERPOWER Vitamin C badass, antioxidant agent

SPIRIT Bianco vermouth, dry sake, dry sherry, dry vermouth, gin, orange liqueur, sauvignon blanc, vodka, white port, white rum

CITRUS Lemon, lime, orange, yuzu

SIDEKICK Coconut milk, coriander, goat's milk, peas, toasted coconut, tomato, vanilla

OOLONG TEA

SUPERPOWER Boosts metabolism, lowers cholesterol, increases mental alertness, aids digestion, stabilizes blood sugar

SPIRIT Amaro, anise, dry sake, gin, mezcal, orange liqueur, pisco, red wine, ruby port, rum (all), scotch, sweet sherry, vermouth (all), vodka, whisky (all)

CITRUS Lemon, lime, orange, yuzu

SIDEKICK Cherries, Chinese five-spice powder, chocolate, cinnamon, coriander, date, honey, lemon oil, maple, orange oil, peppercorns (all), star anise, toasted coconut, vanilla

PARSLEY

SUPERPOWER Rich in phytonutrients, high in vitamins C and K and calcium

SPIRIT Bianco vermouth, chartreuse, dry sake, dry sherry, dry vermouth, gentian aperitif, gin, sauvignon blanc, vodka, white port, white rum

CITRUS Lemon, lime, yuzu

SIDEKICK Black pepper, carrot, cilantro, coriander, mint, smoked salt, tonic water

PLUM

SUPERPOWER Fiber packed, helps absorption of iron, promotes digestion, relieves high blood pressure

SPIRIT Dry Riesling, dry sherry, gin, rosé wine, ruby port, sake (all), vermouth (all), vodka, white port

CITRUS Lemon, lime, orange, yuzu

SIDEKICK Balsamic vinegar, Banyuls vinegar, bay leaf, caramel, coriander, honey, lemon thyme, maple syrup, orange liqueur, pomegranate, rosehips, rose water, smoked salt, ume vinegar, vanilla

POMEGRANATE

SUPERPOWER High in fiber and phytonutrients, antioxidant badass, anti-inflammatory, cancer fighter

SPIRIT Bourbon, brandy, Calvados, gin, red wine (all), ruby port, rye, sake (all), scotch, sherry (all), vermouth (all), vodka

CITRUS Lemon, lime, orange

SIDEKICK Apple, apple cider vinegar, Banyuls vinegar, black pepper, ginger, honey, maple syrup, orange flower water, orange liqueur, pink peppercorn, rose geranium, rose water, sage, thyme, vanilla

REISHI

SUPERPOWER Stimulates brain neurons; fights cancer, autoimmune diseases, and diabetes; relieves asthma and allergies

SPIRIT Brandy, dry sake, dry sherry, dry vermouth, mezcal, rye, scotch, white burgundy

CITRUS Lemon, lime, yuzu

SIDEKICK Amaro, black pepper, celery, honey, mushroom, red pepper, smoked salt, tomato, truffle, wood smoke

RHUBARB

SUPERPOWER Powerful cancer fighter; high in fiber, protein, and vitamins C, K, and B; improves digestion; optimizes metabolism

SPIRIT Aperol, bourbon, Calvados, champagne, Contratto Aperitif/bitter, gentian aperitif, gin, red wine, rosé wine, rye, sake (all), tequila, vermouth (all), vodka

CITRUS Lemon

SIDEKICK Black pepper, coconut milk, coconut water, ginger, pink peppercorn, rose geranium, rose water, strawberry, toasted coconut, vanilla

TURMERIC

SUPERPOWER Anti-inflammatory, antidepressant, pain reliever, combats digestion problems, helps regulate cholesterol

SPIRIT Gin, mezcal, sake (all), tequila, vermouth (all), vodka, white port

CITRUS Lemon, lime, orange, yuzu

SIDEKICK Almond, black pepper, cayenne, coconut milk, coriander, cumin, galangal, ginger, goat's milk, honey, kefir, pepper, raisins, toasted coconut

WATERMELON

SUPERPOWER Antioxidant rich, fights heart disease and hypertension, maintains healthy digestive tract

SPIRIT Aperol, Bianco vermouth, bourbon, Contratto Aperitif/bitter, dry sherry, dry vermouth, gin, melon liqueur, mezcal, orange liqueur, rosé wine, sake (all), sparkling wine, tequila, vodka, white rum

CITRUS Lemon, lime, yuzu

SIDEKICK Aloe vera, basil (all), black olive, cayenne pepper, chile pepper, coconut water, cucumber, jalapeño, mint, orange flower water, pink peppercorn, rose geranium, rose water, strawberry, sumac, toasted coconut, togarashi, tomato

IF YOU BUILD IT,
THEY WILL COME

Once you have mastered making one drink, challenge yourself to make several at the same time. One idea I try to hammer into new bartenders is the importance of building a round—that is, a number of drinks to be served more or less all at once. You've all heard it: "The next round's on me!"

Building any round in a certain order is necessary if you want each drink to be of optimum quality for your guests. If you make drinks in the wrong order, someone will be getting the manky end of the stick. My preference is to build all drinks in their shaking tins or mixing glasses at the same time and consider how the drink will be served before adding ice, shaking, and presenting. The order that follows ensures no one gets the cocktail shaft. The goal is to have all drinks ready within moments of each other:

UP DRINKS (drinks served *without* ice, such as Martinis, Manhattans, and Gimlets) are stirred or shaken and poured first, because there is no ice to melt and dilute them as they wait for the next drink to be made. This type of drink is the most stable and can sit for a few minutes.

DRINKS ON LARGE ROCK ICE (such as Old-Fashioneds and Margaritas) are stirred or shaken and poured next, because the rock ice will melt slowly and dilution will be minimal. This type of drink is slightly less stable than the up drink.

DRINKS ON SMALL ICE CUBES (such as Tom Collinses, Mojitos, and other Highballs) are stirred or shaken next. This drink is much less stable than the up drinks and rock drinks because the small ice cubes dissolve quickly and dilute the drink.

DRINKS ON PELLET, PEBBLE, OR CHIPPED ICE OR FROZEN DRINKS (such as Mai Tais, Juleps, slushy Daiquiris, and smoothie-style beverages) are stirred, swizzled, or shaken and served last. As soon as the liquid hits this small ice, it starts to dilute and deteriorate. This type of drink is the least stable and should wait for no more than a minute before it gets to your guest's lips, less if you are in a hot room or climate.

CHAPTER TWO:
FORAGING

In the last chapter, I covered the necessary items you need for a well-outfitted bar, but that's only the beginning. Here, we gather, prepare, and forage for the essential Clean and Dirty components that make up my go-to arsenal of ingredients I need to start a-tinkering. I rely heavily on a consistent list of staple ingredients that can be found in fancy markets as well as 99-cent stores—I am not a snob and don't discriminate because I never know where my next jolt of electrifying inspiration will come from. I cannot imagine creating drinks without rose water, smoked salt, or vanilla at my fingers.

Living in SoCal, I'm lucky to be surrounded by some of the best and freshest farm-grown produce. The other thing I love about Los Angeles is the wide variety of ethnic food stores here, from the Argentine bodega El Camaguey packed to the gills with all sorts of Latin American goodies, such as purple corn for my version of Chicha Morada (an amethyst-colored fruit punch popular in Peru) to my personal fave, Mitsuwa Marketplace, a Japanese mecca and food hall where I urban-forage for all sorts of unusual delights—among them, steamed lotus root for slicing into slivers of delicate garnish or yuzukosho (a citrusy pepper paste that's an alternative to plain old hot sauce and excellent in spicy Margaritas and Bloody Marys). As we forage on, know that the suggestions in this chapter are by no means exhaustive; if you find something you think might work as an alternative ingredient in one of my recipes, by all means, I encourage you to try it and please drop me a line and let me know how it worked.

JUICES

The difference between freshly pressed or extracted fruit and vegetable juices from carefully selected produce and the concentrated, pasteurized, and otherwise processed crap in boxes and cans is about the same as between wild-caught salmon and cat food. The dilemma originated, I suppose, in the fact that fresh juice is expensive, labor-intensive to make, and can sour quickly. In fact, once citrus juice is pressed, you have a maximum of 24 hours, in my estimation, to use it before it starts to taste off. This is likely why the cheapo stuff was used for so long for everything from Bloody Marys to (that heinous) sweet-and-sour mix. Back in the eighties and well into the nineties—before the full reawakening of whole foods awareness, a commitment to shopping seasonally, and the proliferation of CSAs and farmers' markets—this was effectively all there was in many arenas of bar and restaurant sourcing. Many bought it packaged and attached it to the bar gun along with that other not-so-fresh ingredient, cranberry "juice" cocktail.

The cocktail revolution that began in the early 2000s also did much to propel the comeback of real juice (much to the chagrin of many a lazy bartender), and, along with the whole farm-to-table movement, happily came craft cocktails. By then, there was no longer any way you dared serve canned rubbish alongside your divine plate of Alice Waters–inspired garden-salad tacos.

And as fresh-squeezed juices are essentially raw juices, they retain all their nutritional value—vitamins, minerals etc.—as opposed to processed juices that have most likely been pasteurized via a heat source to give them a longer shelf life, but which destroys both beneficial elements as well as any small amounts of bacteria. The trick is to drink your raw juice within a couple of days, which limits the occurrence of harmful bacteria.

In more good news, getting your fresh fruit and vegetable juices isn't really that hard. There are myriad great tools for the task; following is an overview of the main options. Seek out the ones that match your go-to needs, your pace, your strength, and any pet passions. And always, always be sure to use top-notch produce.

CITRUS JUICERS

Citrus juice may be one of the most underestimated ingredients in great drink making. From a squeeze to a juicy glass of Screwdriver, sparkling-fresh juice from best-quality fruit is essential for a good-tasting libation.

Juicing real live citrus requires the right kind of tools. There is such a selection of gadgets that it can become confusing, especially because you can end up shelling out anything from $20 to $2,000. As you contemplate which route to take, keep in mind how much and what kind of juicing you do. While you can juice citrus with the attachment on your veggie juicer, you cannot juice vegetables in a citrus juicer. So if you love your veggie juicer, you may be set. But if you love orange juice and lemonade and are reluctant to bust out your veggie juicer, you are a good candidate for a dedicated citrus juicer.

SELECTING A JUICER

Citrus juicers work by using pressure to force every bit of juice from between the segments and membranes of these dense fruits via a reamer of some kind. That pressure comes from a machine or our hands. For small amounts, a manual reamer is a must to have around; these store handily, are easy to clean, and can crank out a few ounces in under a minute. A plain wooden reamer that you dig into the fruit is easier than squeezing it with your fist, although you still have to manage the seeds.

The bartender's ubiquitous hinged hand press provides mechanical assistance to make slightly easier work of juicing, and catches the seeds. Remember: as much as it seems to make sense to fit the shape of the fruit to the cup of the juicer, the halved fruit goes into the cup CUT-side down. The reasoning behind it is that the pressure of the reamer forces the maximum amount of juice out with the fruit placed this way, pushing the entire surface of the fruit instead of just the middle portion of it. A tabletop manual reamer does a lot with a few twists and also strains the seeds; fans appreciate that it's less work for tired hands and wrists.

For larger quantities of juice, you have two good options. One is a heavy-duty tabletop mechanical press engineered for super-powerful pressing (this style of juicer looks something like a tiny torture device—which I guess, if you're a lemon, it pretty much is). Ra Chand is my brand of choice in this category.

The second is an electric juicer; these compact, powerful, and fast-working machines do almost all the work for you. While they are the pricier option, they are the bartender's best friend for producing large quantities of juice in a short period of time. My favorite electric citrus juicer, and the most reliable in my experience, is the Waring Pro; it sells for around $150. Cuisinart makes a very affordable electric juicer that costs about $30, but, be aware, it won't be fast enough for commercial use or other juice-centric scenarios.

There is some debate as to which juicers provide the overall best flavor. Some drink-making experts prefer the manual press because, with those, some citrus oils are expelled when pressing the fruit. I personally prefer the electric reamers for the very absence of citrus oil, which I think can be too powerful—a bully for some drinks.

SELECTING CITRUS TO JUICE

When choosing citrus for fresh juice, of course I recommend only buying produce that has been responsibly grown, with minimal human intervention. This doesn't always mean "certified organic." As has become fairly well known, there are small (and bigger) farms out there that aren't able to navigate the rigors of certification for various complex reasons, but choose nevertheless to grow without pesticides or GMOs. Research the extensive and inspiring information online and through other local forums to find the best growers near you.

When selecting citrus fruits, including lemons, limes, oranges, blood oranges, grapefruit, tangerines, and yuzu (and note, many citrus juicers work for pomegranates as well), choose fruit that yields slightly when pressed and feels heavy for its size in your hand. Hard fruits yield minimal juice, so if you store your citrus in the fridge, I recommend pulling it out a couple of hours before juicing to soften, or submerge it briefly in hot water. If you find good-quality citrus with scarred skins, just reserve them for juicing; use unblemished specimens for garnishes, such as wedges and wheels.

FRUIT AND VEGETABLE JUICERS/EXTRACTORS

These powerful juicers are a wee bit more complicated than dedicated citrus juicers. They come in two dominant types, *centrifugal* and *masticating*. Centrifugal models are those you know as the common home juicer; these extract juice by shredding the produce in a fast-spinning mesh chamber made of tiny, razor-sharp teeth. They are affordable—as little as $40—but from my experience and looking at online reviews, I recommend spending $100 or more to ensure better durability and efficiency.

There is some concern that the heat and oxidation created by centrifugal force destroys some of the juice's nutrients. That brings me to the masticating juicer, also called a cold-press juicer. This style of juicer usually has a horizontal design, and squeezes and crushes the food to extract the juice at a slower speed, thus avoiding the heat and oxidization, and ultimately helping retain the maximum amount of good stuff within. However, masticating juicers cost a pretty penny—as much as $500 or more. Fans believe the end product is well worth it; detractors feel they are slow and don't like the fact that many models can't handle larger whole fruits.

If you use a centrifugal machine, the juice that it yields should be drunk within—at most—20 minutes, especially if it's of a delicate green nature (think: spinach, lettuce, or parsley). I like a machine called the Juice Fountain by Breville for small amounts of juice to be consumed immediately. Juices from masticating machines—SKG produces a well-regarded version—usually hold their nutrients and flavor much longer, up to 48 hours in the refrigerator.

Generally either type of juicer/extractor is good for juicing all fruit and vegetables, except maybe berries. Why not berries? Because most are predominantly flesh and completely edible, juicing them leaves behind a large portion of the fruit that could otherwise be consumed. I prefer to blend berries or make consommé from them (see page 58), which extracts more juice. Citrus can be juiced in these machines, although it's best if you peel it before juicing.

SELECTING FRUITS AND VEGETABLES TO JUICE

For both soft and firmer fruits, such as peaches, apples, and pears, choose fruit that is bruise free and yields slightly when gently pressed. Extra-tender fruits, such as raspberries and blackberries, can turn bad quickly, so avoid those with little dark spots or bits of white fluffy mold when choosing them at the market, and use them as soon as possible. When I buy berries, including strawberries, I arrange them in a lidded container, such as a Glasslock, in single layers between paper towels. I've found this is the best way to increase their shelf life.

Vegetables should be firm and seem fresh, like they were just pulled from the ground or picked from the vine; anything sagging or soggy needs to go the way of the compost bin. Check for sand, dirt—even bugs—if the items have come straight from the farm, and give everything a good rinse so you don't end up with unexpected textures or flavors (a nice touch of protein notwithstanding) in your drinks.

BLENDERS

If you don't want to invest in a juicer—and for many preparations either way—a heavy-duty blender is a fine tool for making juices from most fruits, leafy greens, herbs, and nuts, or a combination. The fruit or other food blends into a pulp you can drink as is, turn into your favorite smoothie, or strain for the clearer juice that's best for some recipes in this book.

Regular heavy-duty blenders make short work of soft fruits like berries and ripe peaches, dates, and pears, but with a few extra minutes of spinning, they also do well with things like apples. More powerful models buy you a lot more versatility. My favorite in that category is the Vitamix Vita-Prep for its hardworking capabilities and ease of annihilating fresh roots, such as ginger and turmeric.

To render good-quality blended juice, you will also need these tools:

- Chinois or other fine-mesh strainer to remove pulp and seeds
- Ladle or large spoon to help push the juice through the strainer
- Cheesecloth, muslin, or a nut milk bag for additional straining and clarifying (see following)

CLARIFYING JUICES

Clarified juice is just what it sounds like: clear, pulp-free juice. But why take the time and trouble to clarify? Mostly for reasons of aesthetics and texture. As discussed in Stirring/Mixing (see page 33), drinks with juice are shaken, and drinks without get stirred. However—just to confuse you—it is possible to make a stirred drink with juice. But, for that sought-after ideal unclouded and crystalline look, it's necessary to clarify the juice. There are three methods for clarifying juice to use in drinks where you want a glasslike beauty: centrifugal clarification, agar clarification, and making a consommé.

CENTRIFUGAL CLARIFICATION

The first method is centrifugal clarification. If you have endless amounts of cash, a centrifuge—yes, just like that thing chemists use for particle separation—is for you. Any pulp in the juice is trapped in the filter while the liquid is spun out, kind of like a high-tech salad spinner. A centrifuge will get you beautiful, almost crystal-clear juice, but it's priced out of reach for most us. I have a few colleagues with much larger budgets than mine who swear by this method of clarification; for the rest of us, the methods that follow work just as well with much less expense.

While we are on the subject of salad spinners, however, some people in the bartending community, myself included, do in fact use a salad spinner as a DIY centrifuge. Simply line the basket with a paper towel or a piece of muslin or cheesecloth and pour in the juice. When you spin the spinner, an impressively clear juice runs into the outer bowl. It makes for a pretty nifty trick. This primitive centrifuge works best with juices such as orange, lemon, and lime, and results in fairly good clarity—not quite as good as a real centrifuge or the next two methods, but it does the trick for some purposes, such as making clear punches and flavored ice cubes.

AGAR CLARIFICATION

The second method is for those of you who love science, especially cooking science: agar clarification. In cooking, clarifying broths is often achieved with the help of egg whites. The whites contain a protein called albumin, which attracts the scum (particulates) released from ingredients in a broth. When the proteins bind, they create solid masses that you can spoon off and filter out of the liquid, resulting in a traditional clear consommé. A more compatible coagulant for juices than egg whites is agar, a natural plant-based gelling medium. Just a tiny bit of agar powder does the trick. Though this method, which works best with citrus and pineapple juices, can be time-consuming, it creates some spectacularly clear results. For other fruit and veggie consommés, such as berry, tomato, or rhubarb, read on for a simple twist on cooked consommés. You can find powdered agar online or at your local culinary store.

MAKING A CONSOMMÉ

The third method of clarifying juices is to make a consommé. A fruit or vegetable consommé, while named as such for their consummate simplicity and depth alike, is made quite differently from a broth consommé. In a slow-cooked consommé, you concentrate and clarify the very essence of the food. With juice consommés, brief or no cooking is used to capture the essence in beautifully scented liquids that can be used for any number of drinks. Tomato consommé (also called simply "tomato water") can be used for a plasma-style (lighter-version) Bloody Mary or a variation on a Dirty Martini; you get the full vegetal flavor without the chunkiness. Rhubarb consommé—as well as fellow tart alternatives, guava and strawberry—are excellent in homemade sodas, fruit punches, and stirred cocktails.

AGAR CLARIFICATION

MAKES 2 TO 2½ CUPS [480 TO 600 ML]

Simple and effective, agar will clarify a liquid without congealing it (gelatin clarifies and congeals).

Ice

3¼ cups [780 ml] cold juice

¼ tsp powdered agar

Fill a large stainless steel bowl about two-thirds full of ice. Set aside.

Pour 2¼ cups [540 ml] of the cold juice into a second stainless steel bowl small enough to nestle into the bowl of ice. Set aside.

In a small saucepan over medium-high heat, whisk the remaining 1 cup [240 ml] cold juice with the agar. Bring to a boil, decrease the heat to medium-low, and let simmer for a couple of minutes, whisking occasionally, until the agar dissolves.

Working quickly, pour the agar mixture into the bowl of juice and whisk well. Nestle the smaller bowl into the ice. Set aside and let set for 2 to 3 minutes until coagulated solids starts to form.

Place a fine-mesh strainer or a colander or other strainer lined with cheesecloth or muslin on top of a clean bowl or pitcher. Whisk the set juice mixture so the solids break up—what Dave Arnold (professor emeritus, International Culinary Center) calls "agar curds." Dump the contents of the bowl into your prepared strainer and set aside to allow the liquid to strain off thoroughly, without disturbing it, about 30 minutes.

Once the curds have stopped draining, if you like, you can pour them back into the small bowl and harass them some more with your whisk to release any remaining liquid, and strain again.

Refrigerate in an airtight container where it will last for up to 5 days.

TOMATO CONSOMMÉ

This liquid elegance is delicious quaffed on its own, combined with other juices for a morning wakeup, or in cocktails such as #7 (page 171), or in a stirred Plasma Mary. It can be made using either a cold or a hot method. The advantages of the cold version are a brighter, fresher, more vegetal taste; the cooked version has a far higher yield, but results in more of a cooked tomato flavor.

2 to 3 lb [910 g to 1.4 kg] ripe tomatoes, cored

Place a colander or strainer lined with muslin or cheesecloth on top of a large bowl. Set aside.

Put the tomatoes in a blender and blend on high speed until smooth.

FOR THE COLD METHOD: Pour the blender's contents into the lined strainer. Fold the cloth over the top of the tomato pulp. Place a plate with a heavy weight on top of the cloth to help speed the straining process. Do not otherwise disturb the pulp; if you force it, you won't end up with crystal-clear juice. Carefully transfer the assembly to the refrigerator for about 2 hours, or until thoroughly drained.

FOR THE HOT METHOD: Pour the blender's contents into a heavy-bottomed saucepan and bring to a boil over high heat. *Do not stir.* You want the foam that rises to the top of the liquid to stay at the top, not mix back into the liquid. Once the consommé foams, carefully pour it into the lined strainer. Let it sit on the countertop for an hour or so, until thoroughly drained.

Refrigerate in an airtight container where it will last for about 5 days if stored properly.

NOTE: *With either the hot or the cold method, all that should be left in your strainer is the sad tomato pulp that has been leached dry of all its goodness. The consommé should be a crystal-clear pale yellow color.*

RHUBARB CONSOMMÉ

MAKES ABOUT 4 CUPS [1 L]

Add this bright, rosy pink essence to soda water, champagne, milk-shakes, and smoothies. The vanilla bean adds a soft creamsicle-like flavor; without the vanilla, the flavor is brighter and more fruit forward. You choose which version to make—I suggest making both. This is adapted from a recipe by Michael Voltaggio.

2 cups [480 ml] cold water
2 cups [280 g] sliced rhubarb
1 cup [200 g] cane sugar or coconut
    nectar
Seeds and pod from 1 vanilla bean
    (optional)

Combine the water, rhubarb, sugar, and vanilla seeds and pod (if using) in a large heatproof bowl. Stir to dissolve the sugar and thoroughly coat the fruit with the syrup.

Wrap the bowl in plastic wrap—that is, tightly cover the sides and bottom as well as the top; the goal here is not to leave any gaps where the heating air within can escape. That "steam" from passive cooking is what breaks down the fruit, resulting in a juicy consommé.

Fill a saucepan (one large enough to nest the bowl with the rhubarb on top of) halfway full with water; the water should not touch the bottom of the bowl. Place the wrapped bowl of rhubarb on top of the saucepan and place it over low heat. Bring the water to a very gentle simmer and let the contents of the bowl steam until the rhubarb starts to look soft but still retains its shape. If it cooks too long and turns to mush, your

consommé, though delicious, will be on the cloudier side. Simmer for about 2 hours. Check the water level midway through steaming and add more if needed.

Make sure no steam is escaping from your plastic wrap. If the steam escapes from the bowl you will be left with rhubarb pulp but no liquid—the steam's heat is what coaxes that delicious nectar from the fruit; to prevent steam from escaping, tighten the wrap on the bowl or add another layer. Use oven mitts to handle the hot bowl and protect yourself from any errant steam.

Meanwhile, set up a chinois or other fine-mesh strainer over a large clean heatproof bowl.

Remove the bowl with the rhubarb from the heat and remove the plastic wrap. Be very careful—steam burns! Pour the hot rhubarb mixture into the prepared strainer and let stand for about 1 hour until thoroughly drained. Do not force or stir the mixture as it runs through, or you won't get a clear, smooth liquid. Use immediately, or refrigerate in an airtight container for up to 5 days.

VARIATION #1:
STRAWBERRY CONSOMMÉ

Substitute 2 cups [280 g] hulled and chopped strawberries for the rhubarb. Substitute a few sprigs of fresh lemon thyme or a handful of organic rose petals for the vanilla bean.

VARIATION #2:
GUAVA CONSOMMÉ

Substitute 2 cups [280 g] peeled, seeded, and chopped fresh guava for the rhubarb. Substitute ¼ cup [35 g] allspice berries, whole green cardamom pods, or fresh peeled ginger for the vanilla bean.

NOTE: *The amount of spice might seem excessive but, once mixed into a cocktail, you want those flavors to shine. In my experience, using less spice makes for a far subtler and less interesting flavor. If, however, this tastes too fragrant to you, reduce the amount of spice used. I like to toast the spices in a dry pan over low heat, and crush them in a mortar with a pestle to release more flavor.*

SYRUPS + INFUSIONS

Just the word "syrup" can put the fear of the sickly sweet
into some people. But I'm here to show that—with the right
ingredients—you can make a flavorful, and even healthy, cocktail
without skimping on taste. That puts all kinds of "magical" at
your disposal without any sugary shame. Contrary to what you
might expect, the use of syrup in a drink recipe is primarily as a
unifier—to bring everything together and enhance the flavors of
the other ingredients. It doesn't have to be a lot and it certainly
doesn't have to be sugary sweet; even a splash can mean the
difference between a good drink and a phenomenal drink.

I follow the same logic for infusions: making my own is
less expensive, and I can control the flavor—with no added sugar!

SIMPLE SYRUPS

The most basic of bar syrups, and aptly named, is "simple syrup." It is incredibly easy to make at home, and you should always have a bottle handy. A common formula is equal parts sugar or other sweetener and hot water, stirred together until the sugar dissolves, and cooled. Just like that, your simple syrup is ready to use in any situation where a quick-dissolving sweetener you can add drop by drop and taste by taste is called for. Keep refrigerated in an airtight container for about 1 month.

Following are my recommendations for natural sweeteners to keep in your pantry for simple syrups (or, in some cases, to use undiluted):

- Blackstrap molasses
- Cane sugar, organic, demerara or turbinado, or rapadura
- Coconut nectar, raw
- Date sugar
- Honey, raw (I like Manuka honey, which is full of superfood powers)
- Maple syrup
- Monk fruit
- Stevia

Raw coconut nectar and honey are my two favorites because they are packed with nutrients such as B-complex vitamins as well as potassium and zinc.

Stevia and monk fruit are two plant-based, zero-calorie sweeteners that work well in some drinks—but work with them gradually and carefully, as they can easily be the downfall of others. Both can have an odd aftertaste, so adding too much at once can create a fake-tasting cocktail. I tend to stay away from them for this reason.

Date sugar can be used in the same way as regular processed sugar, it's just less sweet.

When using cane sugar, I recommend organic, demerara or turbinado sugar, and rapadura. White cane sugar is processed to remove all minerals the body needs to digest it, such as magnesium and zinc; these partially processed brown-colored sugars still contain these essential elements, so in small doses they offer some benefit. Coarse-grained demerara sugar registers a hint of caramel on the palate, which makes it perfect for tiki-style and most rum-based drinks. Another name for this light brown sugar is turbinado, more commonly known as "Sugar In The Raw," which is actually partially processed cane sugar. Note that brown sugar is just white sugar with molasses added—don't confuse it with these others. Rapadura sugar is unrefined sugar cane with the cane juice extracted and dried over low heat, which also preserves its natural caramel flavor. While cane sugar makes the most straight-ahead simple syrup, with basically no other flavor than "sweetness," demerara, turbinado, and rapadura make great syrups, too; just be prepared for a different—call it funkier—sometimes earthy flavor.

For ready-made syrup, many turn to agave, thinking a plant-based product, derived from cactus, is a healthier option. I get requests all the time for a "skinny Margarita," meaning made with agave, thinking, naturally enough, it's both healthier and a botanical match with cactus-sourced tequila. The problem is, agave is a bit of a fraud—it has a low glycemic index number, which means it does not spike blood sugar in the short term. However, agave syrup is manufactured with a heat process that destroys all its good sugars and turns them into fructose—a whopping 85 percent, in fact. Therefore, even compared to high fructose corn syrup, agave is arguably the unhealthiest sweetener on the market.

Instead, consider maple syrup or blackstrap molasses. Though I use these rarely, both are flavorful and contain some nutrients. I find they bully other flavors out of my cocktails, though they can be used sparingly to give a drink more nuance. I recommend using no more than ½ tsp of either.

COMPOUND SYRUPS

Compound syrups: just a fancy name for simple syrups with other ingredients added—for every reason from flavor to mouthfeel. Compound syrups are the mainstay of many a cocktail recipe. In my repertoire, whether a Tikka Masala (page 78), Green Tea (page 76), or nut-based syrup (page 80), I reach for them to be inspired, expand the palette, or add an extra layer of flavor complexity. In the recipes that follow, I include slightly varied options for both Dirty (made with the more processed sugars, plus a glug of vodka as a preservative, if you like) and Clean versions. Experiment with your own combos, too; Gum (Gomme) Syrup (page 73), for example, adds automatic richness to a drink and mixes beautifully with juices for, well, simple compound syrups! Try it to taste with pineapple juice or Rhubarb Consommé (page 62).

SPICED SYRUPS

Making syrups and infusions with dried herbs and spices is a little tougher than it is with fresh herbs. Even if you buy your ground spices and dried herbs in small batches, as fresh as possible, at a store where you know the turnover is high (which you should), it still takes more time and special techniques to coax out the flavors.

Whole spices that you grind yourself, pre-ground spices, and ingredients such as brown rice or nuts (as in the Brown Rice Orgeat, page 80), all benefit from toasting to wake them up (stirring constantly over low temperature and being very careful to avoid burning). After toasting, throw any whole pieces into a mortar for pounding with a pestle, or pulse in a clean spice grinder before adding to your infusion, drink, or dish.

The spiced syrups in this section, as with most recipes in this book, come in Clean and Dirty versions. Some of my favorite spices to use in cocktails are coriander, cayenne, cumin, cinnamon, and star anise.

SOUS VIDE

Truth be told, old-school infusing, whether infusing a simple syrup or a liquor (more on that on page 86) with herbs and spices is way too long of a process for me. While I love working with exciting syrups and infusions, I find waiting through their sitting time too hard. Luckily, I was saved by the introduction of the immersion circulator.

Basically, an immersion circulator is a heating coil you place in a water bath in a large pot on the stove top or in a tub on the countertop. The circulator is governed by a thermostat to keep the water temperature constant. Food is placed in the water bath in sealed plastic bags. While the water never boils, the gentle heat of the water bath held steady by the circulator cooks the food with controlled accuracy. The whole technique is called sous vide (French for "under vacuum," referencing the process of vacuum sealing the food before cooking it in the water bath).

Cooking sous vide also greatly speeds the cooking, or the infusion, process—you may get the results you want in as little as 1½ hours instead of 24 hours by conventional methods. Something like homemade bitters, for example, which normally takes 1 to 2 weeks to reach perfection, can be done with the circulator in about 4 hours.

Many fans of sous vide cooking use a machine called a chamber vacuum sealer to seal the food for immersion. I use resealable plastic freezer bags instead; they're much less expensive than buying more pricey machinery. Be sure to use freezer bags for their extra strength, and press out as much air as possible when you seal the bag to approximate the vacuum seal.

If you do want to invest in both the immersion circulator and the vacuum sealer, check out PolyScience's website. They make top-quality home versions that are relatively inexpensive. And if you like the idea of this technique but don't want to buy either, check out the low-tech solution following.

HACKED SOUS VIDE

For all you MacGyvers, there is a way of hacking sous vide. You will need:

- Large cardboard box big enough for the cooler to fit into
- Large bath towel or blanket
- Good-quality insulated cooler, such as Igloo brand
- Pitcher for transporting hot water (and removing cooled water)
- Hot water
- Resealable plastic freezer bags
- Long-stemmed thermometer
- Bulldog clips or other small clamps

Line the large box with the bath towel, letting the ends drape out. Place the cooler in the box.

Pour the hot water into the cooler, filling it about three-fourths full. Place your infusion ingredients (or food) in a resealable plastic freezer bag(s), press out as much air as possible, and seal tightly. Gently place the bags in the hot water bath. Clip the thermometer to the side of the cooler so the probe is immersed in the water. (A digital thermometer with a long wire is a handy choice here; for a clip thermometer, you may have to get clever with tape to affix it to the side of the cooler.)

Close the cooler's lid and wrap the whole shebang in the towel or blanket, securing it with the bulldog clips. Check periodically to make sure the water is at the correct temperature as indicated in the recipe. Remove the cooled water and add more hot water as needed to bring it back to the desired temperature.

BASIC SIMPLE SYRUP

MAKES ABOUT 1 CUP [240 ML]

Simple syrup is wonderfully useful (and to lots of people, surprisingly easy to make). Use it for sweetening everything from iced tea and coffee to smoothies and cocktails. Here are my favorite Clean and Dirty versions. Coconut nectar is less processed and, therefore, cleaner. Because it is a thick syrup similar in consistency to runny honey, it also requires less water to dilute for a good working syrup. While it sits on the Dirty list, processed organic cane sugar is a good go-to for a crystal-clear basic simple syrup.

CLEAN

1 cup [240 ml] coconut nectar,
    or ½ cup [100 g] rapadura sugar
½ cup [120 ml] hot water (see Note)

In a heatproof pitcher, combine the coconut nectar or rapadura sugar and hot water. Stir until the nectar dissolves. Cool before using. Refrigerate, covered tightly, for up to 1 month.

DIRTY

1 cup [200 g] organic granulated cane, demerara, or turbinado sugar
1 cup [240 ml] hot water (see Note)

In a heatproof pitcher, combine the sugar and hot water. Stir until the sugar dissolves. Cool before using. Refrigerate, covered tightly, for up to 1 month.

VARIATION:
SPICED SIMPLE SYRUP

For a spiced syrup, such as cinnamon or cardamom, add ¼ cup [35 g] ground spice to 4 cups [1 L] warm Clean or Dirty Basic Simple Syrup (left). Stir and let sit for 2 to 3 hours to get a full infusion before using.

NOTE: *Hot water for these recipes should be from a boiling kettle, but if you have seriously hot water gushing from your faucet, that can work. I do not cook simple syrups on the stove—all you need is piping-hot water to do the job.*

RAW HONEY SYRUP

MAKES ABOUT 2 CUPS [ABOUT 480 ML]

Raw honey is a good source of antioxidants, antimicrobials, and amino acids that aid digestion and rebalance the gut. Raw honey is clean in that it has not been pasteurized or processed to remove its nutritional value, and it does not have any chemical compounds added to increase its shelf life. Vegetarians, and especially vegans, however, do consider it "dirty" because it is an animal by-product.

1 cup [340 g] raw honey
1 cup [240 ml] hot water

In a heatproof pitcher, combine the honey and hot water. Stir until the honey dissolves. Cool before using. Refrigerate, covered tightly, for up to 1 month.

VARIATION:
CLEAN SPICE-INFUSED RAW HONEY SYRUP

For a spice-flavored honey syrup, add ¼ cup [35 g] ground spices, such as ginger or cardamom, to 4 cups [1 L] warm Raw Honey Syrup. Stir and let sit for 2 to 3 hours to get a full infusion before using. Refrigerate, covered tightly, for up to 1 month.

MISO-MANUKA HONEY SYRUP

MAKES 1 CUP [240 ML]

Miso adds a hint of umami flavor to this rich and aromatic syrup. Use to add a hint of savory in lemonade, hot toddies, or its cold cocktail counterpart, the Penicillin.

1 cup [240 ml] Raw Honey Syrup
    (preceding recipe), made with
    Manuka honey
1 Tbsp sweet white miso
¼ tsp pure vanilla extract

In a blender, combine the honey syrup, miso, and vanilla and blend for about 10 seconds on high speed until smooth. Transfer the syrup to an airtight container and refrigerate, covered tightly, until needed, or for up to 2 weeks.

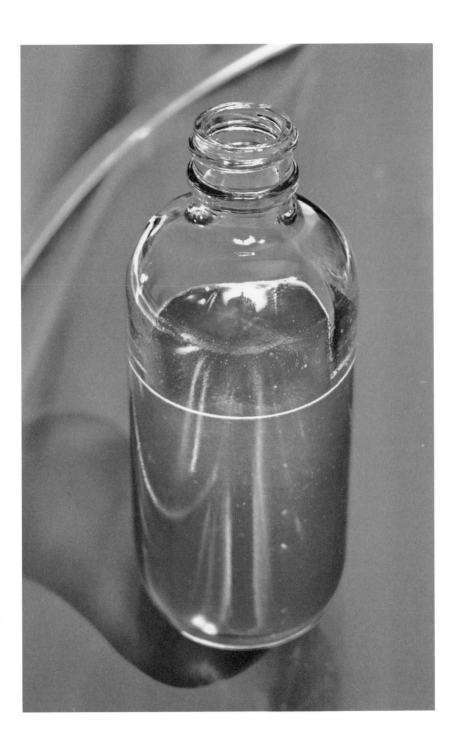

DATE SYRUP

MAKES ABOUT 2 CUPS [ABOUT 480 ML]

This is a tasty alternative sweetener to the highly processed agave syrup for smoothies and mixed drinks. Dates are packed with nutrients and have myriad health benefits, including aiding digestion and helping build bone and muscle strength. They are high in potassium and a great source of energy, so munching on them can give you a preworkout boost. I usually blend them with nut milk as a midmorning treat. Dates and orange flower water are traditional Middle Eastern ingredients that pair beautifully. A splash of the floral water adds refreshing, aromatic notes to the syrup.

10 Medjool dates, soaked for 1 hour in enough warm water to cover, pitted
1¼ cups [300 ml] warm water
1 tsp fresh lemon juice
1 tsp orange flower water (optional)

When the dates are soft, drain well and place them in a heavy-duty blender. Add the warm water and lemon juice. Blend on high speed until smooth and runny, about 20 seconds.

Place a chinois or other fine-mesh strainer over a bowl. Pour the date mixture into the strainer.

Stir the orange flower water into the strained syrup (if using). Let cool before using. Refrigerate, covered tightly, for up to 2 weeks.

NOTE: *This Date Syrup is much less sweet than the Basic Simple Syrup (page 69), so if you're thinking of using it in recipes outside this book, you will need to adjust any citrus called for by half—the usual 1:1 ratio of sweet to sour with date syrup would be 1:½. If you're unsure, add the sour components in increments until you get your desired counterbalance to the date syrup.*

GUM (GOMME) SYRUP

MAKES ABOUT 3 CUPS [ABOUT 720 ML]

Some cocktail recipes call for gum, or gomme, syrup. Gum syrups contain a thickener to produce a silkier texture and richer mouthfeel than other sweeteners. Though we don't use one in this book, it's a great syrup to have on hand for many a cocktail, especially stirred cocktails.

I like to use xanthan gum in my stock gum syrups for the perfect consistency. Classified as a hydrocolloid, meaning it forms a gel in the presence of water, xanthan is a natural substance produced by a bacterial reaction. Bonus: You need very little of it, which is why this recipe makes a big batch by the time you get the right ratio, and it dissolves quickly at any temperature. I've also used food-grade gum arabic, the thickener historically responsible for the name of this concoction, but I prefer xanthan for its ease of use; my other choice is mastic gum for its evocative, pine needle-y flavor.

CLEAN

3 cups [720 ml] Clean Basic Simple Syrup (page 69), warmed to allow for faster absorption of the xanthan gum

¼ tsp xanthan gum

In a blender, combine the simple syrup and xanthan gum. Blend for about 20 seconds until slightly thickened. Transfer to an airtight container and refrigerate for about 4 hours until the syrup is clear before using. Refrigerate, covered tightly, for up to 2 weeks.

DIRTY

Replace the Clean Basic Simple Syrup with 3 cups [720 ml] Dirty Basic Simple Syrup (page 69). Proceed as directed.

GRENADINE

Real grenadine, not that radioactive-looking artificially colored stuff, is a lovely way to add some sweet-tartness to a drink. It's great in everything from lemonade to champagne, pilsner, or soda, to water. This recipe is adapted from one pilfered from bartender-extraordinaire Brian Miller.

CLEAN

4 cups [960 ml] organic unsweetened pomegranate juice

4 cups [960 ml] Date Syrup (page 72)

Peel from 2 navel oranges

1 cup [240 ml] pomegranate molasses (available at Middle Eastern markets; see Resources, page 211)

In a saucepan over medium heat, combine the pomegranate juice, syrup, and orange peels. Bring to a low simmer, stirring to help dissolve the sugar. Adjust the heat as needed to make sure the mixture doesn't scorch.

As soon as the sugar dissolves, remove the pan from the heat. Add the pomegranate molasses and stir until dissolved. Cool before using.

Refrigerate, covered tightly, for up to 2 weeks.

NOTE: *I save my spent orange peels after juicing and use them in place of the orange zest here. Freeze in heavy-duty freezer bags to prevent them from getting freezer burn. Pop them into infusions when orange zest is called for.*

DIRTY

Substitute 2 cups [400 g] turbinado, demerara, or rapadura sugar for the date syrup. Proceed as directed. Stir in 2 Tbsp [30 ml] vodka while the syrup cools, if you like, as a stabilizer and to help the syrup keep for up to 1 month.

HOPS OR GREEN TEA SYRUP

MAKES ABOUT 4 CUPS [ABOUT 960 ML]

Hops are used in beer to add aroma, citrus notes, or bitterness. Outside the brewery, they can be steeped just like a tea—in this case, in a simple syrup where they will impart their unique flavor to anything you like. I use hop syrup most often with citrus, with which it seems to both contrast and mingle in a lovely way; for example, hop syrup with grapefruit juice and soda makes a refreshing nonalcoholic spritzer. Purchase hops online or at your local brewer's shop.

For you green tea lovers, substitute it for the hops in these recipes. Many varieties are similarly flavored to that hops flavor I love—particularly nuanced types, such as jasmine pearl, chai green, or orange blossom. With a tea-based syrup, in just half an hour of steeping, you can turn a boring drink into something with loads of character.

CLEAN

4 cups [960 ml] freshly made Clean Basic Simple Syrup (page 69), warmed

½ cup [70 g] fresh hops, or ¼ cup [35 g] loose green tea, or 4 green tea bags

In a saucepan or heatproof bowl, combine the warm syrup and hops, or tea, and stir to combine. Let stand for at least 2 hours, and up to 24 hours.

Place a chinois or other fine-mesh strainer over a bowl or jar. Pour the infused syrup through the strainer. Use a spoon or pestle to push the mixture through, if you like, but be careful you don't push any bits of hops or tea through, too. Refrigerate, covered tightly, for up to 2 weeks.

DIRTY

Replace the Clean Basic Simple Syrup with 4 cups [960 ml] Dirty Basic Simple Syrup (page 69). Proceed as directed. Stir in 2 Tbsp [30 ml] vodka while the infusion cools, if you like, as a stabilizer and to help the syrup keep for up to 1 month.

SOUS VIDE PREPARATION: *Put the infusion ingredients in a resealable plastic freezer bag(s). Seal tightly, pressing out as much air as possible. Place the bag(s) in a water bath in a large pot with an immersion circulator at 130°F [55°C]. Cook for 1 hour. Or try the Hacked Sous Vide (see page 68) at 130°F [55°C] for about 1 hour. Strain and keep refrigerated, covered tightly, for up to 2 weeks.*

LEMON THYME SYRUP

MAKES ABOUT 4 CUPS [ABOUT 960 ML]

If you're lucky enough to have a garden, or even a window box, grow some aromatic herbs, standout components in all manner of cocktails. Some especially apt herbs for drinks are lemon thyme, parsley, mint, lemon verbena, and lavender.

Soft leaves, such as those on lemon thyme, basil, and mint, can be blanched and puréed into syrups (or spirits; see page 86) in a blender, while the lovely flavors of nonedible leaves and blossoms, such as lemon verbena and lavender, can be steeped like tea, as in the Hops or Green Tea Syrup (page 76).

CLEAN

4 cups [154 g] packed fresh lemon thyme

4 cups [960 ml] Clean Basic Simple Syrup (page 69)

Have ready a bowl of ice water. Bring a saucepan of water to a boil. Add the lemon thyme to the boiling water and stir quickly, just for a few seconds, to blanch. This helps seal in the leaves' bright green color.

Using a slotted spoon, immediately transfer the herbs to the bowl of ice water. Stir until cool. Drain thoroughly in a fine- or medium-mesh sieve.

In a blender, combine the herbs and simple syrup and blend for about 20 seconds on high speed until smooth.

Place a chinois or other fine-mesh strainer over a bowl or jar. Pour the syrup through the strainer.

Refrigerate, covered tightly, for up to 2 weeks.

DIRTY

Replace the Clean Basic Simple Syrup with 4 cups [960 ml] Dirty Basic Simple Syrup (page 69) and proceed as directed. Stir 2 Tbsp [30 ml] vodka into the strained syrup to act as a stabilizer and to help the syrup keep for up to 1 month. Store as directed.

NOTE: *For a flavor variation, use fresh parsley or mint leaves instead of thyme.*

TIKKA MASALA SYRUP

MAKES ABOUT 4 CUPS [ABOUT 960 ML]

Add this syrup—infused with a bouquet of Indian spices—to lemonade, shrubs (see page 108), and all manner of cocktails (see page 209) as well as tea, coffee, smoothies, or even homemade ice cream.

Let this recipe serve as a template for conjuring up mixes of your favorite spices—from cinnamon to sumac. Just keep in mind that syrups such as cinnamon or cardamom need about ¼ cup [gram weight varies] ground spices per 6 cups [1.4 L] of warm Clean or Dirty Basic Simple Syrup (page 69) or Raw Honey Syrup (page 70). Mix the spices into the syrup and let steep for at least 5 or 6 hours before using.

CLEAN

2 tsp ground ginger
2 tsp ground turmeric
1½ tsp ground coriander
1½ tsp ground cumin
1½ tsp ground paprika
1 tsp cayenne pepper
4 cups [960 ml] freshly made Clean Basic Simple Syrup (page 69), hot

In a 1-qt [960-ml] heatproof pitcher or jar, combine the ginger, turmeric, coriander, cumin, paprika, and cayenne. Pour in the hot syrup and stir to combine. Let stand for 2 to 3 hours until very flavorful.

Place a chinois or other fine-mesh strainer lined with cheesecloth or muslin over a large bowl or jar. Pour the syrup through the strainer. Transfer the strained syrup to an airtight container and refrigerate, covered tightly, until needed, or for up to 1 month.

DIRTY

Replace the Clean Basic Simple Syrup with 4 cups [960 ml] Dirty Basic Simple Syrup (page 69) and proceed as directed. Stir 2 Tbsp [30 ml] vodka into the strained syrup to act as a stabilizer and help the syrup keep longer, if you like. Store in an airtight container and refrigerate, covered tightly, until needed, or for up to 1 month.

SOUS VIDE PREPARATION: *Put the infusion ingredients in a resealable plastic freezer bag(s). Seal tightly, pressing out as much air as possible. Place the bag(s) in a water bath in a large pot with an immersion circulator at 130°F [55°C]. Cook for 1½ hours. Or try the Hacked Sous Vide (see page 68) at 130°F [55°C] for about 2 hours. Strain and store as directed.*

BROWN RICE ORGEAT

MAKES ABOUT 8 CUPS [ABOUT 2 L]

Orgeat (pronounced OR-zhat) is a rich syrup made from almonds, sugar, and orange flower water or rose water.

In the cocktail universe, orgeat, and its cousin falernum (included as a variation following), are frequently used in tiki-style drinks, such as Mai Tais or Fog Cutters. Instead of just almonds, I use half almonds and half brown rice, which complement each other nicely. The brown rice is toasted and adds another level of nutty flavor to the delicate almond flavor. You can use all almonds or mix it up as you like; just use 4 cups [about 560 g] of nuts, such as blanched (skinned) hazelnuts (which are quite divine in syrup), pistachios, or even toasted sesame seeds.

Falernum is usually made just from almonds with lime zest and allspice added. It's also a favorite tropical mixer. Where orgeat adds a nutty and floral sweetness, falernum contributes a baking spice and vanilla base note to cocktails. I add it to a spicy Blackberry Margarita or use it as the sweet portion in a simple Tom Collins.

CLEAN

2 cups [380 g] uncooked brown rice

2 cups [240 g] chopped blanched or skinless almonds

Hot water for soaking

8 cups [2 L] Clean Basic Simple Syrup (page 69)

2 Tbsp [30 ml] orange flower water

In a dry sauté pan or skillet over medium-low heat, combine the brown rice and almonds. Cook for about 8 minutes, stirring constantly, until the nuts and rice are fragrant and start taking on some golden-brown color. Be careful not to let them burn. Transfer to a large heatproof bowl and add hot water to cover. Let sit for about 30 minutes to soften.

Strain the rice and nuts through a chinois or other fine-mesh strainer and transfer to a blender. Working in batches if necessary, add the simple syrup. Pulse briefly, just 4 or 5 short pulses. Do not blend—you just want to break up the rice and nuts a little, not pulverize them.

Pour the mixture into a large container with a lid (a standard 1-gal/3.8-L jar works well). Cover tightly and refrigerate for at least 24 hours, or up to 48 hours, for a full, intense flavor.

Strain the syrup through a chinois or other fine-mesh strainer lined with cheesecloth or muslin into a clean large jar or other airtight container. Stir in the orange flower water. Refrigerate, covered tightly, for up to 2 weeks.

DIRTY

Replace the Clean Basic Simple Syrup with 8 cups [2 L] Dirty Basic Simple Syrup (page 69) and proceed as directed. Stir in ¼ cup [60 ml] vodka along with the orange flower water, if you like, as a stabilizer and to help the syrup keep longer. Refrigerate, covered tightly, for up to 2 weeks.

You can also substitute 2 cans [8 fl oz, or 240 ml each] condensed coconut milk (purchased or homemade, see Clean version of Salted Caramel Syrup, page 82) plus an equal amount [2 cups, or 480 ml] water for the 4 cups [960 ml] Simple Basic Syrup.

SOUS VIDE PREPARATION: *Put the infusion ingredients in a resealable plastic freezer bag(s). Seal tightly, pressing out as much air as possible. Place the bag(s) in a water bath in a large pot with an immersion circulator at 130°F [55°C]. Cook for 1½ hours. Or try the Hacked Sous Vide (see page 68) at 130°F [55°C] for about 2 hours. Strain and store as directed.*

HOMEMADE SODA

The Clean or Dirty version of either the Brown Rice Orgeat or the Falernum syrup makes a delicious soda.

2 Tbsp [30 ml] Brown Rice Orgeat (facing page) or the Falernum (see left)
2 Tbsp [30 ml] fresh lemon or lime juice
Ice-cold sparkling water

In a tall chilled glass, combine the syrup and lemon or lime juice. Top with sparkling water for a delightful thirst quencher.

VARIATION:
FALERNUM

Omit the orange flower water. Add ½ vanilla bean, the zest of 2 limes, and a handful of whole allspice berries to the infusion stage of the recipe.

NOTE: *I save my spent lime halves after juicing and use them in place of lime zest in this recipe, and many others. Freeze in heavy-duty freezer bags to keep them from getting freezer burn, and add in place of the zest called for.*

SALTED CARAMEL SYRUP

MAKES ABOUT 1¼ CUPS [420 ML]

Caramel syrup is a wee bit more technique oriented to make than many syrups. It's easy to scorch or splatter, and it can be tricky to tell when the color is just right, or the time reached to set the consistency is just right. You can cheat and buy caramel syrup—I won't judge—but, as with so many things in the kitchen, nothing compares to homemade. The key is to be patient and attentive; I've tried to make these recipes easy for success.

The Clean version (which cuts the calorie count by switching coconut milk for heavy cream) is adapted from a recipe from Wallflower Kitchen, and is amazing on vanilla ice cream and in smoothies and milkshakes. The Dirty version comes from Bobby Flay's recipe for the *New York Times*; it's great on pretty much anything from French toast and bacon to cheese and crackers.

CLEAN

1 cup [240 ml] coconut milk

½ cup [70 g] coconut sugar

½ tsp Maldon smoked sea salt flakes, plus more as needed

1½ tsp coconut oil (I also experimented with sesame oil)

1½ tsp alcohol-free pure vanilla extract

In a saucepan over medium-high heat, bring the coconut milk to a boil. Decrease the heat to medium-low and simmer for about 20 minutes, stirring occasionally, until reduced by half. (You're essentially making condensed coconut milk.)

Add the coconut sugar and salt. Simmer for 2 to 3 minutes more, stirring frequently and scraping the bits off the bottom of the pan with a wooden spoon, until the sauce thickens and turns an amber color.

Remove from the heat and stir in the coconut oil and vanilla. Taste and add a little more salt, if you like. Let cool to room temperature before using. Store at room temperature in a tightly covered container for up to 1 week. If you refrigerate the syrup, it will stiffen up and you will need to allow it to come to room temperature before using. I usually let it sit in hot water to speed the process.

DIRTY

1 cup [200 g] organic cane sugar

¼ cup [60 ml] cold water

½ cup [120 ml] heavy cream

2 Tbsp unsalted butter

1 tsp pure vanilla extract

½ tsp Maldon smoked sea salt flakes, plus more as needed

In a saucepan over medium-high heat, stir together sugar and cold water. Cook for about 10 minutes, without stirring, until the sugar melts and the syrup turns a deep amber color. (You can swirl the pan occasionally, though Chef Flay recommends not touching it until the sugar turns a deep brown.)

Meanwhile, in a second saucepan, gently warm the cream. When the caramel is ready, slowly whisk in the warmed cream in a steady stream. (Be careful, as it will want to splatter when you add the cream.) Return it to a simmer and cook for 2 to 3 minutes

more, stirring frequently, until the syrup is lovely and smooth. You are looking for a deep amber color to tell you it is ready.

Remove from the heat and whisk in the butter, vanilla, and salt. Taste and add a little more salt, if you like. Let cool to room temperature before using. Refrigerate, covered tightly, for up to 1 week.

OOLONG COLA SYRUP

MAKES ABOUT 4 CUPS [1 L]

Growing up in the good old UK, Pepsi was my jam; ironically, it was in the United States that I first had my taste of "Mexican Coke"—Coca-Cola made with real sugar, not the synthetic junk used in mass production responsible for rotting many a tooth. Although, on the upside, you can use it to clean many a tarnished copper pan. (Yes, really. Now think about how it affects your innards!)

I stopped drinking soda—I had one too many fillings and had started getting tweaky on the caffeine. Not until recently did I have a splash of "the Real Thing" and it reinspired me. I started thinking about the possibility of making my own cola syrup, complete with the buzz but without the kill factor. The result is this combination of oolong tea—a cross between green and black tea and chock-full of health benefits—fruits, spices, coconut or date nectar, and a secret ingredient (wait for it)—veggie bouillon!

While both these syrups are way squeaky-cleaner than Coke, I made two versions, a Clean one with date syrup and coconut sugar, and a Dirty one with organic cane sugar. The Clean version is thicker and slightly more vegetal due to the date syrup, but just as delightful; the combo of fruit sweeteners hits all the right spots. A glug of this cola syrup on the rocks topped with sparkling water is a delicious and healthy version of the "real thing."

CLEAN

⅓ cup [11 g] dried oolong tea leaves

6 cups [1.4 L] boiling water

Peel of 2 lemons

Peel of 1 navel orange

2 whole black limes (also called dried limes), available in most Middle Eastern markets (see Resources, page 211)

¼ cup [27 g] dried bitter orange peel, available from most home-brew stores or online (see Resources, page 211)

6 whole star anise pods

4 cinnamon sticks, coarsely chopped or broken (I use a hammer)

2 cups [480 ml] Date Syrup (page 72), or to taste

1½ cups [216 g] coconut sugar, or to taste

Juice of 2 lemons

Juice of 1 navel orange

1 tsp pure vanilla extract

½ tsp vegetable bouillon paste

¼ cup plus 2 Tbsp [90 ml] Tippleman's Burnt Sugar Syrup (optional; see Note)

In a saucepan or teapot, steep the tea in the boiling water for 15 to 20 minutes. Strain the brewed tea into a heavy-bottomed saucepan over high heat.

Add the lemon and orange peels, black limes, bitter orange, star anise, and cinnamon. Bring to a simmer, turn the heat way down to barely a simmer, cover the pan, and let the aromatics infuse the tea for 2 to 3 hours. Strain the infused warm tea into a pitcher or large jar with a lid.

Stir in the date syrup, coconut sugar, lemon and orange juices, vanilla, bouillon, and Tippleman's syrup (if using) until dissolved. Cover tightly and refrigerate overnight and up to 1 week.

DIRTY

Substitute 3 cups [600 g] organic cane sugar for the date syrup and coconut sugar and proceed as directed.

SOUS VIDE PREPARATION: *In a resealable plastic freezer bag(s), combine the strained brewed tea, lemon and orange peels, black limes, bitter orange, cinnamon, and star anise. Seal tightly, pressing out as much air as possible. Place the bag(s) in a water bath in a large pot with an immersion circulator at 130°F [55°C]. Cook for 1½ hours. Or try the Hacked Sous Vide (see page 68) at 130°F [55°C] for about 2 hours. Strain the infused tea into a pitcher or large jar with a lid and proceed as directed.*

NOTE: *I mention the optional use of Tippleman's Burnt Sugar Syrup because it adds a deep caramelized flavor to the syrup base as well giving it a dark-brown color closer to the original sinful Coke. You can also grate the black limes with a Microplane onto fish and chicken dishes to add an invigorating aroma.*

INFUSIONS

It has been a consistent phenomenon in my drink-making career to be working with an owner who wants the best drinks at minimal cost. The bottom line, therefore, has almost always been my bottom line for staying employed. To this end, I realized early on that I would have to save money by not using all those fancy (or expensive) mixers and flavored spirits and make my own infusions instead. I started with a Lapsang Souchong tea–infused spirit that I made into a liqueur—a pretty exotic, or at least ambitious, beginning. But all told, it was a quarter of the price of a store-bought bottle, and the product of my efforts helped me create drinks that had much more integrity and special flavor.

This experience inspired me to make all my own infusions. My pantry (see page 98) became my playground where, to this day, nothing is immune from infusion madness: tea, coffee, spices, fruit, vegetables, nuts, popcorn—you name it, I've tried it somewhere in that index of recipes I carry in my head.

The following section represents a short list of ideas, but I encourage you to extrapolate from here and from your own pantry. Note there is a range of preparation styles here to accompany a range of ingredients.

Most (for example, softer-stemmed herbs, such as mint) can be rendered with an average blender, or even a handheld blender. Other tougher ingredients, such as fresh ginger, may be best reserved for a powerful blender such as a Vitamix. (Again, those will often yield to a decent regular blender; your judgment and experience will lead.) And a number of recipes require no more—or lesser—force than time itself.

SONICATION

The sonicator is a nifty invention (an alternative to sous vide cooking) that helps speed the infusion process. Sonication happens when the gadget produces ultrasonic sound waves that rapidly force molecules to be bashed about at high velocity, similar to a drill bit being put into a liquid and the drill being turned on. As yet, there is not a sonicator on the market that can produce large amounts of infused liquid, so I stick to my sous vide method. However, for smaller projects, the mad scientist at Addiction Mixology makes a sonicator called the Flavor Reactor that sells for under $300, which is great for making homemade bitters.

HOLY BASIL RUM OR PARSLEY VERMOUTH

MAKES ABOUT 3 CUPS [750 ML]

The fresh and heady notes of highly aromatic holy basil make this a must in any refreshing summery cocktail, such as Mojitos, spritzes, and Mai Tais.

4 cups [140 g] fresh holy basil (tulsi) or parsley leaves, blanched (see page 77)

One 750-ml bottle white rum (if using the basil, Cruzan works here) or Bianco vermouth (for the parsley; Dolin Blanc is my preference); save the bottle, if you like, for the infusion

2 Tbsp [30 ml] fresh lemon juice (to keep the botanicals greener longer)

In a blender, combine the basil (or parsley) and rum (or vermouth). Place the lid on the blender and blend for about 20 seconds on high speed until smooth. Strain the liquid through a chinois or other fine-mesh strainer lined with cheesecloth or muslin into a bowl or pitcher. Stir in the lemon juice.

Using a funnel, if needed, transfer the infused spirit to the reserved bottle or other airtight container. Refrigerate, covered tightly, for up to 5 days.

TURMERIC + GINGER SYRUP OR VODKA

MAKES ABOUT 3 CUPS [780 ML]

You aficionados know that ginger syrup is the secret to a good Moscow Mule. For my Indian-inspired version, I use a syrup that combines fresh turmeric and ginger roots—call it a Mumbai Mule (see #23, page 209). A splash of this syrup is delicious in lemonade, a Clean or Dirty spritzer, or Golden Milk, too.

1 cup [100 g] peeled and roughly chopped fresh turmeric

1 cup [100 g] peeled and roughly chopped fresh ginger

3¼ cups [780 ml] Clean or Dirty Basic Simple Syrup (page 69), or one 750-ml bottle vodka (my preference is Mell for its smoothness); save the bottle, if you like, for the infusion

VARIATION: GINGER SYRUP

For a ginger-only syrup or vodka, use 2 cups [200 g] peeled, chopped fresh ginger and omit the turmeric. Proceed as directed.

In a blender, combine the turmeric, ginger, and syrup or vodka. Place the lid on the blender (or you—and your kitchen—will be saffron yellow for days to come!), and blend for 20 to 30 seconds on high speed until the spices are annihilated. Let the mixture sit for 30 minutes.

Using a funnel, if needed, strain the mixture through a chinois or other fine-mesh strainer lined with cheesecloth or muslin into the reserved bottle or other airtight container. Refrigerate, covered tightly, for up to 2 weeks.

BLACK SESAME WHISKEY

MAKES ABOUT 3 CUPS [750 ML]

This nutty and mildly savory infusion adds a fragrant, toasty note to any drink and is great in a Whiskey Sour, Old-Fashioned, or even with a splash of Oolong Cola Syrup (page 84).

½ cup [70 g] black sesame seeds

One 750-ml bottle inexpensive bourbon whiskey, such as Evan Williams or Old Crow; save the bottle, if you like, for the infusion

In a dry sauté pan or skillet over medium heat, toast the sesame seeds for 2 to 3 minutes until fragrant, stirring constantly to make sure they don't burn. Immediately remove them from the heat and transfer to a mortar.

Using a pestle, give the toasted seeds a medium-hard bashing, just enough to break them open. Alternatively, use a second smaller sauté pan or skillet to crush the seeds while they're still in the hot skillet. Scrape them into a large jar and pour in the whiskey. Cover tightly and give it a good shake. Let sit in a cool dark place at room temperature for at least 36 hours and up to 7 days until the whiskey has a full sesame flavor.

Using a funnel, if needed, strain the mixture through a chinois or other fine-mesh strainer lined with cheesecloth or muslin into the reserved bottle or other airtight container. Refrigerate, covered tightly, for up to 2 months.

SOUS VIDE PREPARATION: *Put the toasted, pounded sesame seeds in a resealable plastic freezer bag(s). Add the whiskey. Seal tightly, pressing out as much air as possible. Place the bag(s) in a water bath in a large pot with an immersion circulator at 130°F [55°C]. Cook for 2 hours. Or try the Hacked Sous Vide (see page 68) at 130°F [55°C] for about 2 hours. Strain and store as directed.*

CHAMOMILE VERMOUTH

MAKES ABOUT 3 CUPS [ABOUT 750 ML]

Chamomile adds a soothing quality to any drink or dish, and I don't think it gets used enough. This soothing botanical, combined with honey and citrus, creates a perfect flavor trifecta—at once refreshing, calming, and invigorating. Use it as a mixer for simple Arnold Palmer-style drinks, add it to summery spritzes, or mix it with Scotch whisky for a wintery fireside comforter that works as well hot as a toddy or cold for a sour-style cocktail.

¼ cup [24 g] dried chamomile flowers, or 8 chamomile tea bags

One 750-ml bottle Dolin Blanc, Brovo Pretty, or Martini Bianco vermouth; save the bottle, if you like, for the infusion

In a large jar, combine the chamomile and vermouth. Cover tightly and give it a good shake. Let sit at room temperature for at least 12 hours and up to 48 hours until the vermouth has a full infusion of flavor.

Using a funnel, if needed, strain the mixture through a chinois or other fine-mesh strainer lined with cheesecloth or muslin into the reserved bottle or other airtight container. Refrigerate, covered tightly, for up to 1 month.

SOUS VIDE PREPARATION:
Combine the chamomile and vermouth in a resealable plastic freezer bag(s). Seal tightly, pressing out as much air as possible. Place the bag(s) in a water bath in a large pot with an immersion circulator at 130°F [55°C]. Cook for 2 hours. Or try the Hacked Sous Vide (see page 68) at 130°F [55°C] for about 1½ hours.

NOTE: *Dried chamomile is like a sponge—it will soak up a lot of your liquid. Press out as much liquid as possible when straining. I usually use the back of a small ladle to push the liquid against the strainer. If small pieces pass through your strainer, give it a second straining through a finer CoCo strainer (see page 16).*

GRAPEFRUIT + PINK PEPPERCORN SYRUP OR GIN

MAKES ABOUT 3 CUPS [ABOUT 750 ML]

Artificially flavored spirits are all over the market, but they have nothing on their natural counterparts; what's more, not only are the homemade kinds super easy to make, but nonalcoholic infusions offer a full range of delicious options as well. This unexpected combo is a magnificent mix of sweet, tart, bitter, and spiced.

¼ cup [35 g] pink peppercorns

Peels of 2 or 3 pink grapefruits

3 cups plus 2 Tbsp [750 ml] Clean or Dirty Basic Simple Syrup (page 69), or one 750-ml bottle gin; save the bottle, if you like, for the infusion

In a sauté pan or skillet over medium heat, toast the peppercorns for about 5 minutes, stirring, until fragrant and lightly toasted. Transfer to a mortar and lightly crush with a pestle.

Put the peppercorns and grapefruit peels in a large jar with a lid. Pour in the simple syrup, or gin, and close tightly. Let the mixture infuse for at least 24 hours and up to 48 hours until the infusion is very flavorful.

Using a funnel, if needed, strain the mixture through a chinois or other fine-mesh strainer lined with cheesecloth or muslin into the reserved bottle or other airtight container. Refrigerate the syrup, covered tightly, for up to 2 weeks, or the gin for up to 1 month.

SOUS VIDE PREPARATION: *Combine the ingredients in a resealable plastic freezer bag(s). Seal tightly, pressing out as much air as possible. Place the bag(s) in a water bath in a large pot with an immersion circulator at 130°F [55°C]. Cook for 1½ hours. Or try the Hacked Sous Vide (see page 68) at 130°F [55°C] for about 2½ hours. Strain and store as directed.*

NOTE: *Adding a small amount of sugar to any botanically infused spirit increases the amount of flavor extracted from the product. Via osmosis, the sugar creates an environment in which it strives for balance in the solution, pulling out more of the plant sugars and, with those, more flavor out of the botanicals or spices.*

VARIATION:
KEY LIME

In a large jar, combine 4 cups [960 ml] Clean or Dirty Basic Simple Syrup (page 69), or one 750-ml bottle vodka and 2 cups [500 g] Key limes (6 to 8 Key limes), halved and roughly juiced, peels included. Infuse, strain, and store as directed.

LEMON VERBENA
TISANE OR GIN

MAKES ABOUT 4 CUPS [ABOUT 946 ML]

Tea-like infusions made using plants or spices are called tisanes (see page 103 for more). Here, the scent of lemon verbena is both refreshing and uplifting, and the lightly citrus-scented leaves work equally well in cocktails and desserts. Use with tonic or soda water for a summery Highball or mix with fresh lemon juice and honey in an Arnold Palmer (a mix of lemonade and iced tea).

60 lemon verbena leaves stripped from about 10 stems

4 cups [960 ml] boiling water, or one 750-ml bottle Old Tom Gin, such as Hayman's or Ransom; save the bottle, if you like, for the infusion

Put the verbena leaves in a large heatproof container if you are making the tisane, or a jar with a lid. Add the boiling water, or gin, and close tightly. Refrigerate for at least 12 hours and up to 3 days until the infusion is very flavorful.

Using a funnel, if needed, strain the mixture through a chinois or other fine-mesh strainer lined with cheesecloth or muslin into the reserved bottle or other airtight container. Refrigerate the tisane, covered tightly, for 1 week, or the gin for up to 1 month.

SOUS VIDE PREPARATION: *Combine the verbena and water (use warm tap water, not boiling water), or gin, in a resealable plastic freezer bag(s). Seal tightly, pressing out as much air as possible. Place the bag(s) in a water bath in a large pot with an immersion circulator at 130°F [55°C]. Cook for 1½ hours. Or try the Hacked Sous Vide (see page 68) at 130°F [55°C] for about 2 hours. Strain and store as directed.*

RHUBARB "PIMM'S"

MAKES ABOUT 4 CUPS [960 ML TO 1.2 L]

Pimm's No. 1 is an old-fashioned liqueur made from gin and sweet vermouth infused with caramelized orange, botanicals, and spices using a famously secret recipe—usually two parts vermouth to one part gin. Using this ratio as my jumping-off point, I created my own spin—a light, refreshing, fruity, and vegetal rendition using rhubarb to infuse the gin and vermouth, which has plenty of herbal and spicy notes. The Clean version doubles down on pink by infusing the spring–summer brightness of rhubarb with the unique tart of hibiscus tea. While the original Pimm's is spiced, my version does not use spices because I feel the mix becomes too muddy in flavor, but it is inspired by the same 2:1 ratio.

Because raw rhubarb is quite a hard vegetable, it can withstand a few days of soaking in liquid without disintegrating; leaving it to infuse longer results in a fuller flavor.

CLEAN

5 cups [700 g] diced [1-in/2.5-cm dice] fresh rhubarb

4 cups [960 ml] hibiscus tea or other red fruit tea

Put the rhubarb in a large jar or bowl. Pour in the tea. Cover tightly and refrigerate for at least 36 hours and up to 1 week until the infusion is very flavorful.

Strain the mixture through a chinois or other fine-mesh strainer lined with cheesecloth or muslin into a large bowl. Transfer to a clean large jar or other airtight container. Refrigerate, covered tightly, for up to 2 weeks.

DIRTY

5 cups [700 g] diced [1-in/2.5-cm dice] fresh rhubarb

One 750-ml bottle pink vermouth (Brovo makes the best on the market)

16 fl oz [480 ml] gin

Put the rhubarb in a large jar or bowl. Pour in the vermouth and gin. Cover tightly and refrigerate for at least 36 hours and up to 1 week until the infusion is very flavorful.

Strain the mixture through a chinois or other fine-mesh strainer lined with cheesecloth or muslin into a large bowl. Transfer to a clean large jar or other airtight container. Refrigerate, covered tightly, for up to 2 weeks.

"CAMPARI"

MAKES ABOUT 4 CUPS [1.0 TO 1.1 L]

This bitter infusion is great with soda water for a digestive tonic after too much rich food. For a cold-weather tonic, use whole cardamom pods for a warmer, spicier version in place of the citrus-like notes of the coriander seeds.

CLEAN

4 hibiscus tea bags

3 cups [720 ml] boiling water

¼ cup [35 g] Szechuan peppercorns

¼ cup [20 g] coriander seeds

¼ cup [29 g] juniper berries

¼ cup [27 g] bitter orange peel

Peel of 1 navel orange

1 cinnamon stick, broken into pieces

1¼ cups [300 ml] Clean Basic Simple Syrup (page 69)

1 Tbsp [15 ml] alcohol-free gentian root tincture (see Note, page 161)

In a saucepan or teapot, steep the tea in the boiling water for 15 to 20 minutes.

In a sauté pan or skillet over medium heat, toast the peppercorns and coriander seeds for about 5 minutes, stirring, until fragrant and lightly toasted. Transfer to a mortar and lightly crush with a pestle. Transfer to a large jar with a lid.

Add the juniper berries, bitter and navel orange peels, cinnamon stick, and brewed tea to the jar. Close tightly. Place the jar in a cool, dark place and let sit for at least 8 hours and up to 48 hours until the infusion is very flavorful.

Strain the mixture into a clean large jar or other airtight container and stir in the simple syrup and gentian root tincture. Refrigerate, covered tightly, for up to 2 weeks.

DIRTY

¼ cup [35 g] Szechuan peppercorns

¼ cup [20 g] coriander seeds

¼ cup [29 g] juniper berries

¼ cup [27 g] bitter orange peel

Peel of 1 navel orange

1 cinnamon stick, broken into pieces

One 750-ml bottle inexpensive but
   drinkable dry white wine

1¼ cups [300 ml] Clean or Dirty Basic
   Simple Syrup (page 69)

1 Tbsp [15 ml] gentian root tincture (see
   Note, page 161)

In a sauté pan or skillet over medium heat, toast the peppercorns and coriander seeds for about 5 minutes, stirring, until fragrant and lightly toasted. Transfer to a mortar and lightly crush with a pestle. Transfer to a large jar with a lid.

Add the juniper berries, bitter and navel orange peels, cinnamon stick, and wine to the jar. Close tightly. Place the jar in a cool, dark place and let sit for at least 8 hours and up to 48 hours until the infusion is very flavorful.

Strain the mixture into a clean large jar or other airtight container and stir in the simple syrup and gentian root tincture. Refrigerate, covered tightly, for up to 2 weeks.

SOUS VIDE PREPARATION:

Combine the infusion ingredients in a resealable plastic freezer bag(s). Seal tightly, pressing out as much air as possible. Place the bag(s) in a water bath in a large pot with an immersion circulator at 130°F [55°C]. Cook for 1½ hours. Or try the Hacked Sous Vide (see page 68) at 130°F [55°C] for about 2½ hours. Strain the mixture into a clean large jar or other airtight container and stir in the simple syrup and gentian root tincture. Store as directed.

FROM THE PANTRY

Coming from a family of make-doers and culinary miracle workers, the pantry—or as we call it, the larder—is kind of like my playroom. And so, the market is my toy store. I love nothing more than spending my day off wandering the aisles of Japanese, Indian, and Middle Eastern food stores for hours, marveling like a wide-eyed kid at the choice of condiments, sauces, dried goodies, and jars of pastes and sauces. While it's fun to imagine the magic they add to food, my mind reels with thoughts of how to use them in drinks.

Even the most basic drink recipe or the least expensive spirit can be transformed by your pantry—for example, adding turmeric and ginger to lemonade or infusing a $10 bottle of gin with Earl Grey tea. In the old-school tradition of making something out of almost nothing, with a spoonful here or there, you really can. In most restaurant kitchens, the pantry is stocked with a good selection of salts, dried herbs and spices, oils and vinegars, and other seasonings. In modernist pantries, you are likely to find (all derived from natural sources): xanthan gum to thicken; lecithin, gellan, and Sucro to emulsify and stabilize airs and foams; agar for clarifying, gelling, or foaming purposes; corn maltodextrin for adding density; or tapioca maltodextrin for turning oils into powders (often added to baking or cooking for extra unctuousness). It might sound like bunkum, but add milk powder to your next batch of meatballs—the wonders of the pantry can be life changing. Adding some of these tricks to your drink-making bag can likewise up your game. Try a saltwater foam atop your basic vodka and grapefruit; you may never go back to basic again.

My home pantry also has an obsessive assortment of teas, tisanes, and coffees for the flavors that often become the backbone of my drinks. Next time you're contemplating a peach protein smoothie or a frozen Daiquiri, add a teaspoon of matcha tea powder. You're welcome!

SALT

If sugar is the unifier of a drink, then salt is the brightener. I think of it as fairy dust; in small sprinkles, it can make you fly. That magic touch can also mean the difference between okay and fantastic—it makes chocolate taste somehow more chocolatey, ice cream creamier, and fruit sweeter. It's a bit counterintuitive, I know, but if you are a cook of any kind, you've likely discovered the difference a mere pinch makes to a dish. You can use standard kosher salt or get fancy with sea salt, flaked salt, or salt harvested by Tibetan Sherpas. Each one has a distinct flavor profile. Following is a list of my favorites:

FLEUR DE SEL is made up of hand-harvested salt crystals with a clean, bright flavor; it's great on ice cream and in toffee, caramel, and chocolate.

HAWAIIAN BLACK LAVA SALT is harvested from the Pacific and blended with activated charcoal; it enhances digestive health. Its earthy, mineral flavor is best used as a finishing salt.

HIMALAYAN PINK SALT (you thought I was joking with the Sherpas?) is high in mineral content and has a soft flavor with a hint of sweetness. Its mineral content helps regulate blood pressure and it's a great detoxifier if used in the bath (another time, another book perhaps).

MALDON SEA SALT FLAKES are hand-harvested salt flakes from Maldon, England, with a soft flavor on the palate.

MALDON SMOKED SEA SALT FLAKES, my go-to, are cold-smoked over oak embers, giving the salt subtle smoke flavor. Great with the flavors of caramel, roasted banana, roasted pineapple, coconut milk, mezcal, and grapefruit, to name a few.

SEL GRIS, considered one of the best salts available, is a moist, unrefined sea salt, typically found on the French Atlantic coastal region of Brittany; its naturally occurring gray color is absorbed from the clay ponds it is harvested from. A great finishing salt.

HERBS + SPICES

As a general rule, I don't use dried herbs to flavor a drink. There is one or two I use as a smoked garnish, such as a dried sage or bay leaf that gets set on fire—the fire's heat igniting their aromas. But in general, even if you try to find the freshest bins, many dried herbs are pretty flavorless (and who knows how long they've been sitting). My hands-down preference for drink making is fresh herbs; the flavors are significantly brighter and more distinctive, and you need much less to get a full infusion.

But while I rely heavily on fresh herbs during spring and summer, as the weather gets colder, spice flavors become much more prevalent in my concoctions. In this area, I'm rather promiscuous—I am faithful to no spice and have flings with many. The flavors soon fade with many dried spices as well, though; I strongly recommend toasting them first in a dry skillet to bring them back to life. A quick bashing in a mortar with the pestle further livens them up.

The following list gathers a selection of my favorite aromatic herbs and spices, noting the ingredients and spirits they pair with best.

ALLSPICE Orchard fruit, squash, tropical fruit, amaro, bourbon, red wine, rum (all), sweet sherry, tequila, vermouth (all), vodka

BAY LEAF Root veggies, amaro, dry sherry, gin, Japanese whiskey, Scotch whisky, vermouth (all), vodka, wine (all)

BLACK LIME Tropical fruit, amaro, red wine, rum (all), sake (all), sweet sherry, vermouth (all)

BLACK PEPPERCORN Orchard fruit, squash, tropical fruit, amaro, Calvados, red wine, sake (all), vermouth (all), whisky (all)

CARDAMOM Orchard fruit, squash, tropical fruit, pisco, red wine, rum, sweet sherry, tequila, vermouth (all), vodka, whisky (all)

CHAMOMILE Honey, Japanese whiskey, Scotch whisky, sherry, vermouth (all), wine (all)

CILANTRO Citrus, tropical fruit, mezcal, rum (all), sake (all), tequila, vodka, wine (all)

CLOVES Citrus, orchard fruit, squash, tropical fruit, amaro, bourbon, red wine, rum (all), sweet sherry, tequila, vermouth (all), vodka

CORIANDER Citrus, tropical fruit, gin, Scotch whisky, sherry, tequila, vodka, wine (all), vermouth (all)

CUMIN Citrus, orchard fruit, tropical fruit, amaro, bourbon, red wine, rum (all), sweet sherry, tequila, vermouth (all), vodka

CURRY LEAF Orchard fruit, squash, tropical fruit, Calvados, gin, pisco, red wine, rum (all), Scotch whisky, sherry, tequila, vermouth (all), vodka

CURRY POWDER Citrus, orchard fruit, squash, tropical fruit, Calvados, gin, pisco, red wine, rum (all), Scotch whisky, sherry, tequila, vermouth (all), vodka

FENNEL FLOWERS AND FRONDS Apple, citrus, ginger, dry sherry, gin, sake, wine (all), vermouth (all), vodka

FENNEL SEED Apple, citrus, pear, pineapple, squash, bourbon, pisco, red wine, rum (all), Scotch whisky, sherry, tequila, vermouth (all), vodka

GINGER Orchard fruit, squash, tropical fruit, Calvados, gin, pisco, red wine, rum (all), Scotch whisky, sherry, tequila, vermouth (all), vodka

HARISSA Citrus, pomegranate, rose water, tropical fruit, amaro, dry sake, red wine, rum (all), sweet sherry, vermouth (all)

HOLY BASIL (TULSI) Citrus, tropical fruit, amaro, dry sherry, gin, rum (all), sake, vermouth (all), vodka, wine (all)

KAFFIR LIME LEAF Citrus, tropical fruit, gin, rum (all), sake, vermouth (all), vodka, white wine

LEMON BALM Citrus, dry sherry, gin, sake, vermouth, vodka, white wine

LEMON BASIL Citrus, melon, tomato, tropical fruit, dry sherry, gin, rum (all), sake, Scotch whisky, vermouth (all), vodka, white wine

LEMON THYME Citrus, orchard fruit, squash, gin, sake, sherry, vermouth (all), vodka, wine

LEMON VERBENA Citrus, orchard fruit, dry sake, dry sherry, gin, vermouth (all), vodka, wine (all)

LEMONGRASS Citrus, tropical fruit, dry sake, dry sherry, gin, rum (all), vermouth (all), vodka, wine (all)

NUTMEG Citrus, orchard fruit, squash, tropical fruit, amaro, Calvados, gin, pisco, red wine, rum (all), Scotch whisky, sweet sherry, tequila, vermouth (all), vodka

PAPRIKA Citrus, tropical fruit, gin, Scotch whisky, sherry, tequila, vermouth (all), vodka, wine

PARSLEY Apple, citrus, root veggies, dry sake, dry sherry, gin, vodka, white vermouth, white wine

PEPPERMINT Citrus, melon, tropical fruit, amaro, bourbon, gin, rum (all), sake, Scotch whisky, vermouth (all), vodka, wine (all)

PINK PEPPERCORN Citrus, orchard fruit, rose water, squash, tropical fruit, amaro, bourbon, red wine, rum (all), sweet sherry, tequila, vermouth (all), vodka

RAS EL HANOUT Citrus, orchard fruit, rose water, tropical fruit, mezcal, red wine, rum (all), sake, sweet sherry, tequila, vermouth (all)

ROSEMARY Citrus, orchard fruit, tropical fruit, gin, rum (all), sake, vermouth (all), vodka, whisky (all), wine (all)

SAGE Citrus, orchard fruit, dry sherry, Japanese whiskey, gin, rum (all), sake, Scotch whisky, vermouth (all), vodka, white wine

SHISO Citrus, root veggies, amaro, dry sherry, gin, rum (all), sake, vermouth (all), vodka, white wine

SPEARMINT Citrus, orchard fruit, tropical fruit, amaro, dry sherry, gin, rum (all), sake, vermouth (all), vodka, whisky (all), white wine

STAR ANISE Citrus, orchard fruit, squash, tropical fruit, amaro, bourbon, red wine, rum (all), sweet sherry, tequila, vermouth (all), vodka

SUMAC Apple, citrus, cucumber, fennel, pineapple, dry sake, dry sherry, dry vermouth, gin, tequila, vodka

SZECHUAN PEPPERCORN Citrus, orchard fruit, tropical fruit, amaro, gin, sherry, tequila, vermouth (all), vodka, wine (all), whisky (all)

TARRAGON Citrus, root veggies, dry sherry, gin, sake, vodka, vermouth (all), white wine

THAI BASIL Beets, citrus, melon, tropical fruit, amaro, dry sherry, gin, rum (all), sake, Scotch whisky, vermouth (all), vodka, white wine

TOGARASHI Citrus, tropical fruit, watermelon, dry sherry, rum (all), sake, vermouth (all), vodka, white wine

TURMERIC Carrot, citrus, coconut, dry sherry, rum (all), sake, vermouth (all), vodka, white wine

VIETNAMESE CINNAMON Citrus, orchard fruit, squash, tropical fruit, amaro bourbon, Calvados, pisco, red wine, rum (all), Scotch whisky, sweet sherry, tequila, vermouth (all)

WOOD SORREL Apple, citrus, dry sake, dry sherry, dry vermouth, gin, vodka, white wine

ZA'ATAR Apple, citrus, pear, pineapple, pomegranate, squash, amaro, Calvados, dry sake, red wine, rum (all), vermouth (all), whisky (all)

TEAS + TISANES

As a kid I would drink mugs and mugs of dark brown tea so strong you could stand on it, as the saying went. Our tea was Tetley, the classic black blend—and pretty much the only thing available in stores back then. On rare occasions, as I remember, one might come across some bagged chamomile tea . . . but for the most part, if you wanted anything other than that ruddy brown brew, you had to make it yourself. My Gran Caroline had a garden full of unusual plants—such as feverfew for curing us of stomachaches—but she also grew conventional garden herbs that often ended up in hot tea. These tea-like infusions made using plants or spices are called tisanes; some have health benefits while others are just for flavor. Rarely do they contain caffeine; their properties promote everything from aromatherapeutic relaxation to gut health. Chamomile, chrysanthemum, hibiscus, lemon verbena, and mint all make lovely tisanes. The following are teas and tisanes I often mix with.

BASIL A highly scented tisane exuding earthy, sweet aroma, beneficial for reducing cholesterol and a natural partner to citrus as well as light rum, gin, vodka.

CHAI A warming blend of mixed green, rooibos, and/or black teas with spices; great with tropical fruit.

CHAMOMILE A soothing tisane, great for calming the nerves or for colds; delicious with honey, lemon, Scotch whisky.

CHRYSANTHEMUM This golden-hued tisane, similar to chamomile, is used in Chinese medicine to treat high blood pressure and respiratory infections; mix with raw honey, yuzu, and sake for an elevated version of a hot toddy.

EARL GREY An aromatic tea scented with bergamot orange; great with amaretto (hazelnut), bourbon, gin, lemon, peaches.

GREEN Arguably the healthiest of teas because the leaves are not oxidized like black tea; grassy and refreshing taste. Great with basil, citrus, ginger, peaches, pears.

HIBISCUS A fruity tisane made from hibiscus flowers; great with citrus, mezcal, pomegranate, rose water, rum, tequila.

JASMINE GREEN Green tea flavored with jasmine flowers; great with gin, honey, lemon, lime, sake, vermouth, yuzu.

LEMON VERBENA (OR VERVEINE) This delicate citrus-scented leaf produces a stimulating and refreshing tisane used in cleanses and fasts for aiding in weight loss, protecting muscles, and fighting inflammation; perfect paired with dry gins, sparkling wine.

MATCHA Finely ground powdered green tea; great with basil, coconut, gin, lemon, lime, peach, pear, pisco, rum, sake, vermouth, vodka, yuzu. Also good for baking.

MINT A tisane with digestive properties; great with bourbon, gin, green tea, lemon, maple, vodka.

OOLONG A Chinese tea related to green and black teas and could be said to be, in flavor, halfway between; great with amaro, citrus, rum, spices, sweet sherry, vanilla, whisky.

ROOIBOS A warming caffeine-free red tea made from African red bush; great with brown spirits, honey, lemon.

WHITE A mild tea made from minimally processed leaves; great with bourbon, citrus, gin, honey, rum.

COFFEE

And then there's coffee. . . .
Though I am not a big coffee drinker, the flavor is great to mix into cocktails. I usually pair it with other ingredients, such as chocolate, cinnamon, caramel, and orange oil, or spirits such as sweet sherry, amaro, and mezcal. I think good coffee flavor should be nutty without the bitter aftertaste. The best flavor comes from fresh-ground beans within two weeks of their roasting date; after that, the beans start to lose their oils and get a bit flat. Ground espresso and slow-drip cold brew are my two favorites for mixing with; the flavors are much brighter and shine better in mixed drinks. While it may be tempting to use good-quality instant coffee at a busy bar, it really should be avoided (although it can be great for baking). Whole coffee beans are also great for spirited infusions; the next time you want to make an Espresso Martini, consider making your own coffee liqueur (see page 86 for inspiration).

OILS (FATS) + VINEGARS

Think these ingredients should just be relegated to your salad bowl? These not only have the power to add great depth of flavor to cocktails, but they are also great tools for altering mouthfeel. Let me explain.

When you use a higher-proof spirit, as much as you may love its characteristics, too much "heat" in a drink can make it unappealing on the palate. By heat, I mean that hot, burning finish of most booze. The majority of spirits are 80 proof, which translates to 40 percent alcohol by volume (ABV). The heat in those spirits burns out fairly quickly with dilution and the addition of sweeteners, citrus, etc., which balances them amicably. Less expensive spirits, the ones I mostly infuse and tinker with, while great for my budget, can pack a hot kick, as can higher-proof spirits, like my Gran's Polish Spiritus or a long-barrel-aged whiskey, which can come in at proofs of 100 or higher. These types of spirits are prime candidates for combining with an ingredient that contributes some mouthfeel adjustment. First: oil, or fat.

OILS (FATS)

Believe it or not, oils and other fats—every sort from olive to nut to butter—are subtle but very useful ingredients for adding balance to a shaken or blended cocktail. They work for Clean or Dirty versions, softening the high-heat burn of alcohol or imparting another level of flavor and unctuousness. Be careful to choose a fresh, better-quality oil that sings brightly. To enlist oil (and fats) in balancing a drink, use only small amounts dropped into cocktails, such as whipped sours, flips, or blended smoothies, or via a rather remarkable trick called fat-washing.

Fat-Washing

Fat-washing is a technique whereby a liquid fat, such as brown butter or nut butter, is melted into another liquid (in our case, a spirit or syrup) to "wash over" the molecules. Because the fat and water, or alcohol, don't mix, the fat does not actually infuse the spirit or syrup. The process of fat-washing occurs when the liquid fat molecules "coat," or bind, with the spirit or syrup molecules, imparting flavor and softening its texture (which is more noticeable in spirit washing because the fat masks the imperfections of less expensive spirits and helps remove phenols in aged spirits). Once the fat does its job, removing it is fairly easy. In the case of butter, the melted fat is solidified to separate it from the host liquid it was cozying up to.

How does this work, you ask? In basic terms (though it's still rather miraculous), when the fat adheres to the molecules in the liquid, it delivers a generous amount of texture and flavor. The separation and removal process removes the majority of the fat. So the process adds flavor and texture but does not add a whole lot of extra calories from the fat.

Common fats I use for fat-washing are brown butter, coconut butter, coconut oil, and goat's milk. I've also tinkered with chicken fat and beef drippings, but they have less viable applications in my cocktail lexicon, so I don't play with them often (colleagues have used chorizo fat and bacon fat, too).

Following are my suggestions for pairing my eight essential fats with their best counterparts. Always choose fresh, high-quality oils that sing brightly. Note: Most nut oils go rancid very quickly, especially in a hot kitchen, so refrigerate once opened.

BROWN BUTTER Apples, autumn spices, bananas, bourbon, brown rice, Calvados, caraway, nuts (all), pumpkin, raisins, rum (all), sweet potato, sweet sherry

COCONUT BUTTER Apples, autumn spices, bananas, bourbon, brown rice, Calvados, caraway, nuts (all), pumpkin, raisins, rum (all), sweet potato, sweet sherry

COCONUT OIL Allspice, basil, bourbon, chai tea, cilantro, cinnamon, lime, nuts (all), rum (all), Scotch whisky, star anise, sweet potato, tropical fruit, yuzu

HAZELNUT OIL Allspice, basil, bourbon, cilantro, cinnamon, lime, nuts (all), popcorn, rum (all), Scotch whisky, star anise, sweet potato, tropical fruit, yuzu

NUT BUTTER Amaretto, banana, berries, bourbon, cayenne pepper,

chocolate, dried fruits, fruit spreads, honey, rye, tahini

OLIVE OIL Apples, bourbon, dark rum, grapes, miso, pears, raisins, Scotch whisky, sesame, stone fruit, sweet potato, sweet sherry

SESAME OIL Aged sherry, amaretto, banana, bourbon, cayenne pepper, chocolate, ginger, honey, Japanese whiskey, maple syrup, pineapple, rye, Scotch whisky, turmeric

WALNUT OIL Apples, bourbon, brandy, Calvados, grapes, pears, raisins, rum (all), rye, Scotch whisky, sesame, stone fruit, sweet potato, sweet sherry

MILK

It may be surprising to find milk included with fats, but it is essentially fat and water—be it animal fat or nut or grain oil. Back in the nineties all that was available was soy milk or that dishwatery rice milk. Since then, rice, soy, hemp, and nut milks have become ubiquitous; any good supermarket offers an extensive selection of dairy-free alternatives, and natural foods stores have been fully stocked long before, of course.

As with fat-washing, milk can also be used to temper the ABV "heat" of a spirit (see page 105). Whereas fat-washing adds texture and flavor, milk-washing uses the milk solids to bind with and "wash out" unwanted compounds in a liquid, such as phenols and tannins. To achieve this, lemon juice is added to curdle, or bind, the solids in the milk, which then act like a magnet and attract those aforementioned compounds. Both are then carefully removed.

Milk has its role in mixology—either incorporating it into a drink (consider cream in an Alexander cocktail or Ramos Fizz) or used in a washing process as just discussed.

Milk-Washing

Milk-washing, invented in the 1800s and often used in pre-Prohibition milk punches, became a popular way to soften the flaws of inexpensive and harsh spirits. It works particularly well in tea-infused spirits, which leave behind a bucketload of wicked tannins that can result in an unbalanced cocktail. The milk is added to the tea-washed spirit, followed by small amounts of lemon juice, which causes the milk to curdle; the curds attach to the tannins and suck them out of the liquid. Most recipes call for full-fat cow's milk; I have more success and achieve a softer mouthfeel using goat's milk. (While I do not include a milk-washed drink in this book, you can learn more about this method from Dave Arnold's book, *Liquid Intelligence: The Art and Science of the Perfect Cocktail*.)

VINEGARS

The usefulness and impact of vinegar in drinks is lesser known. In stirred boozy drinks without citrus, vinegars can add the perfect tart foil—you may not know it, but your favorite sip may include balsamic, apple cider, or Banyuls vinegar, or *verjus* (the juice of unripe grapes or crabapples—technically not a vinegar at all but

you get my point: good-tasting acid). Vinegars can also be substituted for citrus in homemade sodas, and are essential in the tart syrups called shrubs (see page 108).

Following is a list of vinegars my pantry would feel Old Mother Hubbardish without, paired with their best counterparts:

APPLE CIDER Apples, beets, blackberries, bourbon, brandy, Calvados, fennel, ginger, mulberries, rosehips

BALSAMIC Amaro, chocolate, dates, figs, hibiscus, pomegranate, raisins, rum, strawberries, sweet sherry, sweet vermouth, whiskey

BANYULS Amaro, bourbon, chocolate, Concord grapes, dates, Kyoho grapes, pomegranate, raisins, red wine, rum, sweet sherry, sweet vermouth

CHAMPAGNE Brandy, citrus, dry sherry, dry wine, gin, green grapes, green tea, peaches, pears, pisco, plums, vodka, white vermouth

RICE WINE Celery, citrus, cucumber, dry sake, dry sherry, dry vermouth, gin, green grapes, tomatoes, vodka

UME Citrus, dry sherry, gin, pomegranate, raspberries, red wine, rose water, strawberries, stone fruit

WHITE BALSAMIC Apple, celery, citrus, cucumber, dry sake, dry sherry, elderflower, fennel, gin, green grapes, raspberries, stone fruit, vodka, white vermouth, white wine

SHRUBS

Q: When is a shrub not a leafy green bush?

A: When it's a Colonial precursor to the modern-day soda.

Confused? I understand; it's a bad joke but a good new trend for an old notion—or rather, potion.

Shrubs are all the rage right now, found in handsome bottles on the shelves of cool shops and farmers' markets everywhere right next to artisan bitters. They add a depth of flavor and nuance to a cocktail that citrus cannot because its flavors are less complex.

The name and the concept come from a seventeenth-century fruit liqueur made by mixing rum or brandy with sugar and citrus peel. Popular among sailors, shrubs provided a way to use foul-tasting spirits when there wasn't much else on board.

The soft-beverage version was a method of extending the shelf life of summer fruits far into the winter months. Fruit was mixed with sugar and acidulated with a complementary vinegar (see list, page 107). The resulting tart syrup was added to carbonated water for a refreshing fruit soda.

The most common recipe for those sea-faring times seems to have been three equal parts fruit to sugar to vinegar. Call me a landlubber, but I personally feel that's too sharp a flavor, so I cut the vinegar by half, or more—for a really tart vinegar, such as apple cider, my ratio would be 1:1:½.

Shrubs, so easily made and quickly aged but with a deep range of flavors, really deserve their renaissance. I love that you can make them with fruits and also sweet veggies such as beets and fennel. Plus, the addition of a complementary herb or spice can really elevate a shrub to something incredibly special. For me, aromatic shiso, a member of the mint family, is the perfect partner to earthy beets and makes any drink it's used in shine brighter. In addition to their delightful place in a cocktail, shrubs are also great drizzled over ice cream or creamy desserts, or just added to soda water for a bracing soft drink.

FERMENTED BEVERAGES

All vinegar is produced using fermentation, a process that converts sugar into acid or alcohol. Two popular tart fermented beverages are kombucha and water kefir. Both contain beneficial probiotics to aid digestion and both work well in Clean or Dirty cocktails.

Kombucha is basically fermented tea that's produced when yeast and bacteria are introduced to the tea. The "scoby," or symbiotic culture of bacteria and yeasts, is introduced to the liquid in a cloth-covered vessel, allowing for native yeasts in the air to permeate and aid the scoby on its mission.

Water kefir is similar in that a culture of yeast and bacteria is responsible for fermenting the liquid, except it works on sweetened water or juice. It is not as astringent as kombucha and does not contain any caffeine. The same method is needed for fermentation of water kefir grains to occur; native yeasts in the air contribute to this process.

Both fermented beverages can be used to mix drinks as a replacement for any sparkling beverage called for—be it soda water, beer, champagne, or cider.

Note that to do this, everything you use must be *immaculately clean*, *sterilized*, and *stored at the correct temperature*. Fermentation, when not controlled, can be disastrous and make you really sick.

BROWN BUTTER–WASHED SYRUP OR RUM

MAKES ABOUT 8 CUPS [2 L]

Use this syrup in sours, or the rum in Daiquiris, as well as in the banana-based cocktail (#16) on page 192.

1 lb [455 g] unsalted butter, cut into cubes

8 cups [2 L] Clean or Dirty Basic Simple Syrup (page 69), or two 750-ml bottles of your favorite rum

In a saucepan over medium heat, melt the butter. It will start to foam; give it a stir occasionally to make sure it's not burning. After 6 to 7 minutes, once you see little dark specs of caramelized solids at the bottom of the pan, keep a very watchful eye on your butter; it can rapidly turn from nutty amber brown to burnt and useless. Keep stirring until the foam turns light brown and you smell a nutty aroma, 1 to 2 minutes longer. Swirl the pan to make sure you have a good amount of browned bits at the bottom. If you don't, place it back over the heat until you do, still stirring occasionally. Remove from the heat and let cool.

Pour the syrup, or rum, into a 1-gal [3.8-L] jar or other airtight container. Add the cooled brown butter and secure the lid tightly. Give the jar a good shake and place it in a large heatproof, watertight container such as a large stockpot. Fill with hot water and let sit for at least 1 hour or up to 4 hours, during which time the butter melts and adheres, or coats, the syrup or rum molecules.

Remove the butter mixture from the hot water bath and refrigerate until the brown butter solidifies on top. Once solidified, remove the butter disk and save it for another use (French toast, frosting, and banana bread would all be good ideas!). You may need to strain off some smaller bits of fat with a slotted spoon or small strainer. Transfer the butter-washed syrup or rum to a clean jar(s) and refrigerate, covered tightly, for up to 2 weeks.

SOUS VIDE PREPARATION: *Brown the butter as directed, cool, and put it in a resealable plastic freezer bag(s). Add the simple syrup or rum. Seal tightly, pressing out as much air as possible. Place the bag(s) in a water bath in a large pot with an immersion circulator at 130°F [55°C]. Cook for 2 hours. Or try the Hacked Sous Vide (see page 68) at 130°F [55°C] for about 2 hours. Let cool, remove the fat, decant the liquid into a clean jar(s), and store as directed.*

BROWN BUTTER–WASHED BANANA RUM

This is delicious used in Mai Tais, Piña Coladas, Daiquiris, and even in baking.

Brown the butter as directed. Mash 6 ripe bananas into the brown butter while it's still in the pan. (This is pretty much Bananas Foster rum; the hot butter cooks the bananas and brings out their natural sugars.) Put the banana-butter mixture into a 1-gal [3.8-L] jar or other airtight container and add the rum. Set aside at room temperature—do not use the heated water bath method. Let stand for at least 24 hours and up to 48 hours until the infusion is fully flavored.

Strain the liquid well (if you don't, it will be nearly impossible to remove any banana solids from the liquid once it's cooled). Transfer the strained liquid to a clean container and refrigerate until the brown butter solidifies on top. Once solidified, remove the butter disk. Because the banana and fat stick together in this instance, the butter is not good for reuse here.

COCONUT BUTTER–WASHED SYRUP OR SCOTCH WHISKY

MAKES ABOUT 6 CUPS [1.4 L]

Coconut oil and coconut butter are readily available in well-stocked supermarkets and natural foods stores. The oil is extracted from the nut whilst the butter is made by grinding the nut pulp into a paste. I reuse the butter disk for another batch of washed whisky or syrup—it has enough flavor for one more wash.

1 cup [220 g] coconut butter

6 cups [1.4 L] Clean or Dirty Basic Simple Syrup (page 69), or one 750-ml bottle Scotch whisky

Put the coconut butter in a 1-gal [3.8-L] jar or other airtight container. Add the syrup or whisky and secure the lid tightly. Give the jar a good shake and place in a large heatproof, watertight container such as a large stockpot. Fill with hot water and let sit for at least 1 hour or up to 4 hours.

Remove the coconut butter mixture from the hot water bath and refrigerate until the fat solidifies on top. Once solidified, remove the fat disk and save it for another use. You may need to strain off some smaller bits of fat with a slotted spoon or small strainer. Transfer the coconut butter–washed syrup, or rum, to a clean jar(s) and refrigerate, covered tightly, for up to 2 weeks.

BROWN RICE OR NUT MILK

MAKES ABOUT 8 CUPS [2 L]

Use this in place of regular milk most everywhere, including smoothies and shakes and baking (though I advise removing baked goods from the oven sooner than recommended in the recipe as the fat content in plant-based milk is much lower), and it's great for making drinks #16 (page 192) or #20 (page 202) from this book. Be forewarned: This can sometimes curdle when added to drinks with larger amounts of citrus.

2 cups [400 g] uncooked brown rice or [240 g] chopped blanched skinless almonds

8 cups [2 L] hot water

8 cups [2 L] filtered water

In a dry sauté pan or skillet over medium-low heat, cook the rice or almonds for 5 to 10 minutes, stirring constantly, until fragrant and starting to take on some golden-brown color, being careful not to burn. Transfer to a large heatproof bowl and add the hot water. Let sit for 30 minutes to soften.

Strain the rice or almonds through a chinois or other fine-mesh sieve and transfer to a blender. Working in batches, if necessary, add the filtered water. Pulse briefly, just 4 or 5 short pulses. Do not blend—you just want to break up the rice or nuts a little, not pulverize them. Pour the

mixture into a large container with a lid (a standard 1-gal/3.8-L jar works well). Cover tightly and refrigerate for 24 hours or up to 3 days until the milk has a really full, intense flavor.

Strain the liquid through a chinois or other fine-mesh strainer lined with cheesecloth or muslin into a clean large jar or other airtight container. Refrigerate, covered tightly, for up to 2 weeks.

SOUS VIDE PREPARATION: *Follow the toasting instructions as listed. Put the toasted rice or almonds in a resealable plastic freezer bag(s). Seal tightly, pressing out as much air as possible. Place the bag(s) in a water bath in a large pot with an immersion circulator at 130°F [55°C]. Cook for 1½ hours. Or try the Hacked Sous Vide (see page 68) at 130°F [55°C] for about 3 hours. Strain and store as directed.*

BEET + SHISO SHRUB

MAKES ABOUT 2 CUPS [480 ML]

I'm a big fan of root veggies, especially carrots and beets. Their sweet, earthy flavors tantalize my taste buds, whether in a salad, my morning juice, or mixed into a cocktail. The process of making a beet shrub is similar to that of a fruit shrub—the beets are infused in the vinegar, imparting a deep and tasty character perfect for the season and the beer it is paired with in drink #13 (page 185). You can also mix in about 2 fl oz [60 ml] soda water or champagne for a bracing spritz.

½ cup [50 g] peeled and sliced fresh ginger

2 large beets, golden or red, scrubbed

2 Fuji apples

1 cup [200 g] organic cane sugar or [240 ml] Date Syrup (page 72)

6 fresh shiso leaves or sweet basil leaves

¼ cup [60 ml] apple cider vinegar, or to taste

Run the ginger and beets through a juicer. Add the apples. The apple juice will flush out any remaining flavor in the juicer. Strain the juice into a jar with a lid.

Stir in the sugar and shiso leaves. Add the apple cider vinegar in increments, tasting as you go, until you reach your desired acidity level. Secure the lid tightly and shake well.

Refrigerate for at least 12 hours while the sugar dissolves and the shiso infuses. Keep refrigerated, covered tightly, for up to 2 months. Remove the shiso leaves before using.

NOTE: *I think juicing makes this recipe far easier to make. If you don't own a juicer, grate the beets, ginger, and apples and proceed as instructed. The steeping time will increase by about 2 days (and the grating process is a little messy!). Strain out the solids when you're happy with the flavor. Refrigerate to maintain the freshest flavor.*

PLUM AGRODOLCE OR SWEET + SOUR SHRUB

MAKES ABOUT 2 CUPS [480 ML]

Agrodolce, in Italian, translates to sour (*agro*) and sweet (*dolce*) and is often made into a condiment that is used with roasted meats to balance the fat. I use mine as a chutney-esque dip with cheese sticks or to top creamy desserts as well as mixed into sodas and cocktails. This eponymous stone fruit shrub works just as well with peaches or apricots.

1½ lb [680 g] black plums, pitted and chopped

2 cups [480 ml] unsweetened pomegranate juice

½ cup [170 g] honey, plus more as needed

¼ cup plus 2 Tbsp [90 ml] ume plum vinegar or white balsamic vinegar, plus more as needed

6 green cardamom pods, crushed

1 tsp black peppercorns

½ tsp kosher salt

Juice of 1 lemon

Sterilize two 1-qt (1-L) jars, or one ½-gal (1.9-L) jar, and their lids by submerging them in boiling water for 10 minutes. Remove and use immediately.

Divide the plums between the jars.

In a nonreactive saucepan over high heat, combine the pomegranate juice, honey, vinegar, cardamom pods, peppercorns, and salt. Bring to a boil, lower the heat, and simmer for 10 minutes.

Remove from the heat and stir in the lemon juice. Taste and adjust the flavor with more honey or vinegar as needed. Divide the liquid between the jars, leaving 1 in [2.5 cm] of space at the top. Secure the sterilized lids. Refrigerate for 2 to 3 days before using.

GINGER + MANUKA KOMBUCHA

MAKES ABOUT 14 CUPS [3.5 L]

Kombucha can be an acquired taste. For some people, it's a little too astringent. To me, it adds a lovely dry accent to finish off a fruity spritz or a hoppy, floral Shandy. You can reuse your scoby until it starts to get too "dirty"—it will pick up debris such as tea leaves, etc. I've reused mine up to ten times. A scoby will also reproduce at some point.

Gather together the following equipment to make this recipe: one 1-gal [3.75-L] sterilized Mason jar, clean kitchen towel or muslin, elastic bands, and two 2-qt [2-L] clean glass jars.

14 cups [3.5 L] filtered water

1 cup [200 g] organic cane sugar

8 ginger tea bags

2 white tea bags

2 cups [480 ml] starter tea (this can be store-bought kombucha)

1 scoby (check brew shops or online; see Resources, page 211)

1 cup [340 g] Manuka honey

Four 3-in [7.5-cm] pieces fresh ginger

In a large saucepan over high heat, bring the filtered water to a boil. Remove from the heat and add the sugar, stirring to dissolve. Add the tea bags and infuse for 1 to 2 hours until the water cools.

Remove and discard the tea bags. Pour in the starter tea and transfer the liquid to the large sterilized Mason jar and, with clean hands, add the scoby. Cover the jar with a clean kitchen towel or muslin and secure it with elastic bands. Store the jar at room temperature and out of the sun. Ferment for 7 days.

After 7 days, taste with a spoon. You want it to be tart; if it's not, keep fermenting, tasting every day. If you're happy with the flavor, start the bottling process.

Divide the honey and ginger between the two jars. With clean hands, remove the scoby and place it in a clean bowl. At this point, start a new batch of kombucha (if you don't start another batch immediately, the scoby has nothing to live in/on and dies), repeating the steps listed.

Pour the kombucha, straining if needed, into the jars, leaving about 2 in [5 cm] of space at the top. Secure the lids and shake to dissolve the honey. Store the bottles for 1 to 3 days at room temperature, out of direct sunlight, until carbonated. When you're happy with the fizz level, move the kombucha to the refrigerator to stop fermentation (and avoid explosions). Consume within 1 month.

VARIATION:
STRAWBERRY + HIBISCUS

Use 1 pt [280 g] strawberries in place of the ginger, and hibiscus tea in place of the ginger tea.

COCONUT WATER KEFIR

MAKES ABOUT 4 CUPS [946 ML]

Coconut water to kefir grains (which look like large bath salts before they are rehydrated) is like catnip to cats—they love it and thrive on the water; however, don't use the kefir grains in coconut water repeatedly or they will start to lose their vigor.

Gather together the following equipment to make this recipe: one 1-gal [3.75-L] sterilized Mason jar, clean kitchen towel or muslin, elastic bands, chinois or other fine-mesh strainer, and one 1-qt [946-ml] plastic soda bottle with cap.

4 cups [960 ml] coconut water (preferably fresh, not packaged)

1 Tbsp [14 g] prepared water kefir grains (that have been soaked in sugar water to wake them up, see Note)

Pour the coconut water into the sterilized Mason jar and add the kefir grains. Cover the jar with a clean kitchen towel or muslin and secure it with elastic bands. Store at room temperature, out of sunlight, for 48 hours. Coconut water ferments quite quickly, so taste it frequently. If it tastes sour, it's overfermented and should be discarded.

Strain the liquid and, using a funnel if needed, transfer it to your clean soda bottle. At this point you can add some flavorings or juices; mint and pineapple are my obsession, but for our featured recipe we need it unflavored. Leave at least 2 in [5 cm] of space at the top of the bottle, secure the cap tightly, and store it out of the sunlight until carbonated. The beauty of the plastic bottle is it will fill with gas and turn rock solid, letting you know it's ready. Refrigerate to stop the fermentation. Consume within 1 month (mine lasts a day or so).

NOTE: *Dissolve ¼ cup [50 g] sugar in 3 to 4 cups [720 to 960 ml] hot water. Let it cool to between 68°F and 85°F [20°C and 29°C] before adding the water kefir grains. You can also follow the package instructions on the grains, or online at Kombuchakamp.com.*

EMULSIFIERS

The definition of an emulsifier is a substance or compound that stabilizes emulsions to stop liquid separating—egg yolks are used in mayonnaise to stop the oil from detaching from the vinegar. Egg whites also act as emulsifiers and thickeners, but egg yolks, or any fat for that matter, should not be introduced into an egg white–emulsified drink because the fat from the yolk renders the power of the white useless.

EGG WHITES

Here's a bit of science for you: Egg whites are made up of proteins that change when you heat them, beat them, or mix them with other ingredients. You've heard that egg whites are pure protein—well, these proteins are made up of globular chains of amino acids (long chains curled like a party horn). These proteins drift around peacefully in the water that surrounds them, but when you apply heat, or bash them around, say, in a shaker, they knock into each other, their strands uncoiling and connecting with other strands. In between these strands, air is trapped, making the whole solution light and fluffy.

I frequently have guests at my bar asking to eliminate the egg whites from a drink because of dietary requirements or being squeamish about drinking raw eggs. I, of course, oblige but explain that the proteins in the whites help soften the burn of the spirit in the drink. Much like fat-washing (see page 105), the protein in the whites mellows everything out. Is there a substitute that's veggie based, I hear you asking—why yes, yes, there is!

AQUAFABA

I recently trained a bartender who is vegan and refused to touch egg whites when she was making drinks—a problem, because I use whites a fair amount behind the bar. And, I couldn't help thinking it was too bad she would never know how delightful an egg white sour drink tasted.

With this in mind, and because I get numerous vegan drinkers at my bar, I looked into possible ways of making an egg white–like drink without animal products—and without spending a ton of moolah on modernist ingredients. The Vegan Society was my main source of information. On their website, I found recipes for vegan marshmallows and meringues, which seemed pretty much impossible to me without egg whites. They offered a great, "new-ish" discovery for mimicking the function of egg whites in cooking science: aquafaba—literally "bean water." It turns out that the liquid from cooking legumes is full of proteins and starches that make it a great vegan substitute for egg whites. A reliable and easy source is found in the liquid in a can of organic no-salt-added chickpeas; 2 Tbsp [1 fl oz, or 30 ml] of aquafaba is the equivalent of 1 large egg white.

I tested the chickpea water on a well-known drink writer here in Los Angeles and she could barely tell the difference. To me, it actually tasted better—no sulfur-tinged "wet dog" smell of egg whites as I went to sip my delicate, fluffy drink. My vegan challenge was solved and I was converted! Actually, I no longer use egg whites behind any of my bars, both because aquafaba works cleaner and because it is plant based.

You'll find that my recipes often use aquafaba as a key ingredient and other times list it as an optional dash. In the former case, it is because the emulsifier works to soften either a spirit or a tannin, plus a full head of foam makes a great surface to float a garnish on; in the latter, add a splash for texture to liven up an otherwise flat surface.

NOTE: *It's crucial to remember that when creating drinks containing aquafaba, or egg whites, the emulsified mixture must be strained into the glass as soon as it's shaken; otherwise, the foam loses air and starts to separate from the drink, making it less lush.*

MODERNIST INGREDIENTS

Modern gastronomy and mixology use ingredients that change the property of a liquid, either turning it into a foam, gelling it, or helping dehydrate it. All these powders are themselves made from naturally occurring substances. I only use a small selection of these ingredients, to whip up a booze-laden foam or to thicken, clarify, or gel.

Agar Agar Agar agar (sometimes labeled "super agar" on commercial brands) is a gelling agent derived from seaweed. I use it primarily for clarifying (see Agar Clarification, page 57), but also for creating dissolvable stock cubes for hot toddies and for fluid gels. If you mix it with a nonacidic solution, use about the same amount of agar as you would gelatin. However, if using it with a high-acid solution, you need about 1 to 2 grams [0.3 to 0.7 oz] more. Choose a non-GMO version for best results.

Lecithin Lecithin, as with egg whites, is an emulsifier used to stabilize air and bubbles. It's water based, so it cannot be used with alcohol.

Sucro This is another emulsifier used for foaming spirits.

Xanthan Gum Another thickener that I use for making Gum (Gomme) Syrup (page 73). It dissolves in either hot or cold liquids, but cannot be cooked.

HOT TODDY STOCK CUBES

MAKES ABOUT TWENTY-FOUR 1-INCH [2.5-CM] CUBES

I developed this sweet version of stock cubes a few years ago whilst working for *Top Chef* alum Michael Voltaggio at his Los Angeles flagship restaurant Ink. It was a particularly cold winter (ahem . . . below 60°F [15.5°C]) and we were getting frequent requests for hot toddies. As we did not have access to a steamer nozzle or room for a hot plate behind the bar, it was a bit of a challenge during a busy service to oblige. I had seen Chef Amanda Cohen make frozen stock cubes of veggie goodness for her stir-fries that dissolved once added to a pan. That got my mind whirring: How could I do the same thing with a hot toddy? And so this agar stock cube was born.

1½ cups [360 ml] fresh lemon juice

½ cup [120 ml] water

1¼ tsp agar agar

¾ cup [180 ml] Miso–Manuka Honey Syrup (page 70)

¾ cup [180 ml] Ginger Syrup (page 89), Clean or Dirty; up to you

3 Tbsp [45 g] cane sugar or Date Syrup (page 72)

Vegetable-based cooking spray

24 whole cloves

¼ cup plus 2 Tbsp [90 ml] reishi tincture

24 [1-in, or 2.5-cm] lemon peels (peel the rind into strips before you juice the lemons so you don't waste anything; you can also use a Microplane to zest the lemon instead of cutting strips)

In a saucepan over medium heat, combine the lemon juice and water. Bring to a simmer and whisk in the agar agar. Turn the heat to the lowest setting and continue whisking until the agar dissolves fully. Remove from the heat and transfer to a pitcher.

Stir in the honey and ginger syrups and let cool slightly. Stir in the cane sugar, or date syrup, and cool further.

Meanwhile, place two silicone ice cube trays onto a sheet pan or cutting board. Evenly coat the inside of each cube mold with cooking spray and wipe out any excess with a paper towel.

Add 1 clove, ¾ tsp reishi tincture, and 1 lemon peel to each cube.

Once the agar mix is cool, pour it slowly into the ice cube trays to fill. The agar will set without refrigeration, but because you are using perishable ingredients I recommend refrigerating this for at least 12 hours and up to 48 hours.

To use, gently run a palette knife around the edges of each cube. Flip the tray over and coax the cubes out of the mold.

NOTE: *For a boozy version, substitute 1 cup [240 ml] whiskey for the ½ cup [120 ml] lemon juice and the ½ cup [120 ml] water. Add ½ cup [120 ml] Drambuie or Pimento Dram.*

DATE FLUID GEL

MAKES ABOUT 2 CUPS [480 ML]

I was making a drink a while back that called for a schmear of marmalade on top of a thin seed-bread cracker. Great idea in theory but spooning it on was not the most logistically sound way to make the garnish, so the fluid gel was born. It's a much cleaner way of adding a dollop of sweet, jammy goodness to that crisp, rather fragile raft because it's piped out of a squeeze bottle for a faster and more efficient method. This is also delicious on dried fruit or cheese.

Gather together the following equipment to make this recipe: heavy-duty blender (I recommend Vita-Prep), small rimmed metal sheet pan, flexible rubber spatula, squeeze bottle with a lid, and gram scale.

CLEAN OR DIRTY

1 cup [240 ml] fresh orange juice

¾ tsp agar agar

1 cup [240 ml] Date Syrup (page 72), or amaretto for a Dirty version

¾ tsp alcohol-free almond extract (if not using amaretto)

¼ tsp vanilla bean paste, or vanilla extract for a Dirty version

In a saucepan over high heat, bring the orange juice to a boil. Whisk in the agar agar until it dissolves fully. Remove from the heat and stir in the date syrup, or amaretto, almond extract if not using amaretto, and vanilla. Pour the mixture onto a sheet pan and refrigerate until set.

Once chilled, scrape the agar gel off the pan and into a blender. Blend on high speed until smooth. You have the option of passing this through a fine-mesh sieve to eliminate any lumps, but this recipe comes out quite smooth. Pour into a squeeze bottle and refrigerate before using.

FINISHING TOUCHES

I was taught the art of the finishing touch by two master crafts-people. The first, a Holocaust survivor from Poland, Koppel Kandelzucker, was an intensely funny, yet understandably melancholy, man who reminded me of another Polish Holocaust survivor, my Pops. Mr. Kandelzucker was a gentlemen's tailor, whom I trained with for some time in the NW3 neck of London's woods. In the beginning, he would fret over my hand-stitching, chiding me with, "Do it right or get out." I was tormented by him to create the perfect hand-stitched lapel that would effortlessly roll like a petal from the jacket. He insisted on the Goldilocks method of the "just right" amount of tension in my thread for best results. He also showed me French seams and the discipline of clean stitchwork on both the right and the wrong sides of the garment, and the proper way to sew on a button (another "wax on, wax off" moment—I spent hours waxing thread, sewing, and resewing).

The second was my printmaking professor, Elaine Brieger, who obsessed with me over composition and editing, adding or removing elements of visual noise, or the tireless blending of color.

The finishing details—whether on a hand-tailored suit or a piece of visual art—are essential to a masterpiece's success (not that we're creating masterpieces, but it's the same with drinks). Sure, you can make a simple Martini with a wonky twist—it will taste just about the same—but add a little finesse to that twist, trimming its edges into a perfect yellow ribbon and that simple drink becomes enticingly sexy.

COMPOSITION, OR YOU EAT WITH YOUR EYES FIRST

In music, literature, or art, the concept of composition refers to the arrangement, or creation, of a work. The way a drink is presented need not be a monthlong study, but you do need to look at how best to present any given drink for maximum exposure of its ingredients. For instance, if you have a highly aromatic drink, consider using a glass or vessel that traps the aromas and forces the nose into the glass as it is sipped. This is, of course, important with wines and brandies, but also with teas, cocktails, and spirits.

When I use a leafy garnish, I try to get a bit Zen and pare it down to the simplest arrangement, rather than overwhelm the glass and the drinker. Drinking your cocktail should not be like looking for a needle in a haystack. In fashion, those little hats that sit jauntily cocked on many a royal's head are called "fascinators." As pretentious as it may sound, I like to think of my garnishes in the same way—a dramatic gesture placed for maximum effect.

A garnish should also complement the theme of a drink. When I'm inventing drinks, I try to stick with one theme—whether its color, culinary culture, flavor family, or story-line. For example, I made a drink with bee pollen: Pollen comes from bees; honey comes from bees; chamomile goes with honey; honey goes with lemon. The spirit that made sense in this line of thought was Scotch whisky, which often has subtle honey notes (here complementary to the bee pollen) depending on how it has been aged. The bee pollen is but a wee sprinkle on the top, the scent of which enhances the sum total flavor of the drink.

In my design-school days, our brief was often to take a classic item and deconstruct it—to make it new. So, when reimagining classics such as a Piña Colada, rather than blend everything together I will separate the coconut milk (which, instead, sits on top as a foam). Perched on this sits the fascinator—a fragrant kaffir lime leaf that plays beautifully with coconut milk. Coconut water also flavors the drink. These ingredients add layers of flavor, and the following sections describe some of my favorite ways of achieving this layered effect.

Tool	Use for
atomizer	spritzing aromatics or bitters
channel peeler	skinny citrus twists
dropper bottles	precision drops of liquid
Japanese vegetable cutters	fun floral shapes
mandoline (see page 17)	ultra-thin slicing
paring knife	precision cutting
single-hole punch	decorating twists and slices
spiralizer	skinny veggie strings
squeeze bottle	piping fluid gels
tweezers (see page 19)	precision placement
Y peeler (see page 19)	stripping larger pieces of citrus peel
zester or Microplane (see page 18)	finely grating citrus zest, cheese, nutmeg

AROMA

Just as the finishing touch to your morning ablutions is often a spritz of something alluring, aroma plays a vital part in adorning a drink. Yes, you eat with your eyes first, but you taste with your nose second. Classic drinks oftentimes are finished with the oils from an orange, grapefruit, or lemon twist, or a misting of absinthe or flamed bitters. In contrast, some modern drinks I've made were decked out with wood smoke, tobacco smoke, smoky scotch mists, frankincense, Douglas fir, bacon aroma, or balsamic vinegar. As long as the scent plays into your drink's personality, why not add to the total experience?

The simplest way to scent a drink is with a citrus twist. The twist, sheared off a fresh lemon, orange, or grapefruit, is held above the drink and then pinched so its oils are released, falling onto the drink and the glass rim. The twist is then rubbed onto the rim for further flavor.

You can go one step further and flame the twist. The fire intensifies the oil's flavor. This works best on orange twists because they have more oil to share in their skin. To do this, simply hold a lighter beneath the twist and pinch it. Again, rub the twist on the rim of the glass.

Flaming also works on bitters. Because of their high alcohol content, they light up beautifully. Transfer some bitters into an atomizer. Hold a lit match near (in front of) the drink and spritz the bitters toward the drink and match, making sure the spritz hits the flame.

Absinthe, another high-proof spirit, can also be set afire. For a classic tiki-style offering to the gods, pop a sugar cube into a spent lime half and douse it in absinthe. Place the lime on top of the drink and light it up. Once the flame dies down, the absinthe and sugar cube are dropped into the glass.

Fire's close relation, smoke, also adds another element to your creations. Your source can be as simple as a barbecue wood chip or as fancy as frankincense or a smoking gun packed with pipe tobacco. When using the wood chip or frankincense, you will need a fireproof surface such as a piece of slate or marble. Place the chip or lump of resin on the surface and light it. Let the flame envelope the smoke's source and then upturn a glass over the top, starving it of oxygen and trapping the smoke. Whilst the glass gets smoked, mix your drink. Once ready, swish the drink around in the glass and allow it to pick up those smoky nuances.

The smoking gun method requires a wee bit more effort. The "gun" acts on the same principle as a chimney: Air is pumped into the flaming substance and funneled through a pipe into your glass or container, where your liquid is taking a nap. To trap the smoke, wrap the vessel with plastic wrap, giving it one-on-one contact with the liquid. You can add wood chips, tea leaves, bay leaf, or tobacco to the chamber.

And lastly there are smoke-tinged spirits, such as an Islay whisky or mezcal, which you can add to your spritzing gadget. Islay is distilled from barley that has been smoked over burning peat. The barley picks up a range of earthy, as well as oceanic, notes. Mezcal is made from agave plants that have been fire-roasted and pick up a distinct smoky bouquet. For some folks, both spirits can be incredibly overpowering mixed into a drink, where they can bully out more delicate flavors. A quick spritz adds aroma without the overwhelming campfire smell.

Aroma can also come from botanicals. The most-used garnish behind the bar is fresh mint. It gets a quick smack to release its oils before gussying up the top of your drink, though it's not just about being frou frou. The idea is that the mint should hit your nose as you dip to drink—yes, it's there for a bit of colorful variety, but it's also a crucial element to drinks such as Juleps, Mai Tais, and Mojitos. Even plain old lemonade benefits from its attendance in the glass.

But why just stick to mint when there is a garden full of plants begging for consideration? My current favorite sprigs are rose geranium, Thai basil, and lemon verbena. Try them in a glass of fresh strawberry lemonade and be transported to a summer idyll in the south of France (at least that's where my head goes). For more pairings, check out the Heroes, Superpowers + Sidekicks section (see page 41).

There is also a range of food-grade scents available from Aftelier (Aftelier.com) in Berkeley, California. Mandy Aftel, the genius mastermind behind the business, is one of the world's most dedicated all-natural perfumers who creates award-winning perfumes, as well as culinary aromas. A little goes a long way so, to me, it's well worth the cost. My favorites are apple, pear, lemongrass, galangal, and frankincense.

BRINES: PICKLED OR LIQUORED

Regardless of whether you soak your ingredients in alcohol or vinegar, the process is the same. You will, however, use two different "brines": one made with vinegar, salt, herbs, and/or spices, the other a mixture of booze, sugar, and herbs or spices. The ingredients need to be prepared exactly the same—the cherries or olives pitted; the kumquats halved; the grapes or tomatoes peeled. The reason for this is they all have skins or membranes that make it difficult for the liquid to penetrate.

With all ingredients, look for firmer unblemished produce that can take a bit of soaking. You don't want them falling apart mid-infusion. Tomatoes should be the bite-size cherry variety; grapes should be seedless. To peel either, place them in a small strainer. Dunk the strainer into a pot of boiling water for 3 to 4 seconds and quickly transfer it to a bowl of ice water. The skins should now peel off pretty easily. Olives should be firm—I love Castelvetrano olives for their texture and mild flavor. They also stand up nicely to cooking abuses. Green strawberries can be found at your farmers' market. They are simply not-yet-ripened strawberries. I also pickle fresh nasturtium seeds. They have a lovely spicy green flavor and are great with a splash of fine dry vermouth or sherry.

THE OUTER EDGE

Rimming a glass with salt is commonplace for drinks such as a Margarita, or spices for a Bloody Mary. A classic Lemon Drop cocktail or, in some cases, a Sidecar will get a sugar rim to balance the tartness. The purpose is to add another layer of flavor. But why stick to the same old when there is such a bevy of dried powdery things to have fun with?

As mentioned before, I spend a good deal of time skulking around the aisles of many ethnic food markets. My favorite finds in my local Japanese market are shichimi togarashi (a powdered blend of chiles, orange peel, poppy or cannabis seeds, seaweed flakes, and sesame seeds), furikake (dried anchovy, seaweed flakes, salt, and sesame seeds), li-hing (a salty and sweet plum powder), ume salt (dried Japanese plums and salt), and matcha salt (powdered green tea and salt). Most contain some ingredients such as MSG and processed sugar. If this does not bother you, then, by all means, gussy up the rims of your drinking glasses.

Middle Eastern markets have a plentiful array of spice blends, such as the North African ras el hanout (roughly translated as "head" or "master of the shop"), which is a blend similar to the Indian garam masala. Ingredients vary depending on who's mixing it. It is generally more of an aromatic spice blend than a hot one.

SWEET-TART POWDER

MAKES ⅖ CUP [100 G]

You can add a rim of spicy pepper to a simple lemonade for variety, but one of my current favorite rims is the sweet-tart rim (think: sour patch candy for your glass). Though not available commercially, it's fairly easy to make yourself—all you need is cane sugar and powdered citric acid.

Gather together the following equipment to make this recipe: gram scale and a small Mason jar [½ pint, or 240 ml] with lid.

2 Tbsp [20 g] powdered citric acid
6 Tbsp [80 g] evaporated cane sugar
(coconut sugar works too but is
darker and more earthy tasting)
Lemon wedge for preparing the glass

Place the citric acid and cane sugar in a small Mason jar. Secure the lid and shake well to incorporate the powder and sugar.

To use: Pour about ¼ cup [37 g] onto a saucer (this is usually enough to rim 2 glasses). Rub a lemon wedge around the rim of your glass and dip the rim into the powder.

Store in an airtight container in a dry place with a silica packet inside to absorb any moisture.

HERB OR FLOWER HYDROSOLS

YIELD VARIES, BUT USUALLY EQUALS ABOUT
HALF THE AMOUNT OF WATER YOU START WITH

A hydrosol is a scent that is suspended in a water (hydro) solution. These are more common in Middle Eastern cooking than in Western cooking. Orange flower water and rose water are both hydrosols. Making your own hydrosol is fairly simple and uses common kitchen tools and ingredients, such as pots, pans, and ice. The most effective scents are achieved using strongly scented botanicals, such as peppermint, lavender, rose geranium, rosemary, etc. Dispensed from atomizers, it is a clean spritz to finish off your creations.

6 oz [170 g] scented botanical leaves or flowers
Water (enough to almost cover the botanicals)
2 scoops of ice (at least 4 cups [1 L])

Place a wire rack or upturned heatproof ramekin in the bottom of a large stockpot or soup pan. Set a heatproof pitcher or bowl on top of the stand or ramekin.

Add the botanicals to the bottom of the pot and almost cover them with water. Place the lid on the pot upside down. Fill the upturned lid with ice.

Place the pot on the stove and turn the heat to low. Heat the water to a low simmer, warm enough to steam the botanicals but not cook them. As the steam rises, it hits the lid and condenses against it because of the cold ice. The droplets fall into the pitcher or bowl below—this is your hydrosol. Store in an airtight container or atomizer.

CLEAN PICKLING BRINE

MAKES 4 CUPS [960 ML]

This aromatic version of pickle juice features star anise, which adds a depth of flavor that complements the kumquats' sweet-tart flavor. It also works well on cherries for a savory variation on the classic cocktail garnish.

¼ cup [44 g] mustard seeds

4 bay leaves, preferably fresh

2 star anise pods

1 Tbsp Szechuan or black peppercorns

3 cups [720 ml] rice wine, apple cider, or champagne vinegar

1 cup [240 ml] Clean Basic Simple Syrup (page 69) or Date Syrup (page 72)

In a dry skillet over medium heat, toast the spices until you start to smell their aroma. Transfer the toasted spices to your mortar and give them a brief bashing with the pestle to open them up and increase their surface area. Toss the spices into a 1-qt [960-ml] Mason jar.

Add the liquids. Secure the lid and let marinate for at least 12 hours before using. This will keep, refrigerated and covered tightly, for up to 2 months.

NOTE: *Alternatively, speed the process up by cooking via sous vide (see page 67): Cooking at 122°F [50°C] for 2 hours should do the trick. Store as directed.*

VARIATION:
PICKLED KUMQUATS

Inspired by the classic sweet-and-sour sauce with a hint of fragrant aromatics, these pickled kumquats can be muddled in a savory smash or thirst-quenching lemonade. This recipe makes 2 cups [300 g].

Add 2 cups [300 g] halved kumquats to 4 cups [960 ml] Clean Pickling Brine. To infuse the kumquats, follow the same procedure for Drunken Cherries (see facing page). These will keep, refrigerated and covered tightly, for up to 1 month.

DIRTY DRUNKEN "BRINE"

This is not so much a brine as a sauce to get your cherries "sauced." This syrup and spice-fortified brandy works just as well if you substitute chocolate or cherry liqueur for the simple syrup portion. Bonus that it can be reused once you've devoured your cherries.

10 allspice berries

6 green cardamom pods

1 cinnamon stick

½ vanilla bean

3 cups [720 ml] inexpensive brandy

1½ cups [360 ml] Clean or Dirty Basic Simple Syrup (page 69)

In a dry skillet over medium heat, toast the allspice berries, cardamom pods, and cinnamon stick until you start to smell their aroma. Transfer the toasted spices to your mortar and give them a brief bashing with the pestle to open them up and increase their surface area. Toss the spices into a 1-qt [960-ml] Mason jar.

Add the vanilla bean and liquids. Secure the lid and let marinate for at least 12 hours before using. This will keep, covered and refrigerated, for 1 month.

VARIATION:
DRUNKEN CHERRIES

Crunchy bites of fruity goodness burst with flavor. Use these in classic Manhattans or on top of a swirl of dark chocolate ice cream. This recipe makes 2 cups [310 g] cherries.

Add 2 cups [310 g] pitted cherries to 4 cups [946 ml] Dirty Drunken "Brine." To infuse the cherries, add them to the jar at the same time you add the spices and let everything infuse together, or wait for the brine to get a bit more fragrant before adding them. They need to infuse for at least 48 hours. If you choose to go the sous vide route (see page 67), the job can be done in 4 to 5 hours at 122°F [50°C]. These will keep, refrigerated and covered tightly, for up to 2 months.

TASTY GARNISHES

Garnishes run the gamut from a simple lemon wheel perched on a rim to tasty edibles—mini bites that can be served with a drink. Why should the Bloody Mary have all the fun with its buffet of edibles? One favorite at Birch (a Los Angeles restaurant for which I developed the drinks menu) is an Old-Fashioned riff, mixed with brown butter and marmalade. Traditionally the garnish is an orange twist and, perhaps, a cherry depending on where in the country you might be. The garnish on this current iteration is a sliver of seeded bread with a schmear of orange marmalade and a Drunken Cherry (page 131)—craftily getting my quota of orange and cherry in there.

Other edible garnish options include a Parmesan Frico (page 137) on a lettuce drink, playing into the whole Caesar salad thing, a sesame rice cracker with a dollop of date jam on a tahini shake, candied cranberries on a Cape Codder or Cosmo, or a dehydrated blood orange slice on a wintery spiced red wine punch.

Edibles can be grouped into two categories: *animal*, meaning anything that comes from one of God's creatures—bacon chunks, cheese crisps, bee pollen, or a schmear of lardo—or *vegetable*, meaning any kind of plant life, such as apple slices, tomatoes, peppers, or edible flowers. We could add *minerals* as a category and turn this into an intro for Twenty Questions, but the lone ingredient here would be salt. There are other edible minerals out there, such as bentonite and calcium, but, as yet, I have not figured out how to trick them out for a drink.

TASTY GARNISHES: ANIMAL VARIETY

You've heard the saying "Butter makes it better"? This should be my motto (though half my diet is controlled, conscious, and healthful, the other half is devilishly decadent and indulgent; I rely on osmosis to balance both sides). Butter, I think, is what heaven tastes like. It's just not fair that it's also loaded with calories, so I can't munch on sticks of it. Butter (or other animal fat) lends a garnish a delicious mouthfeel as well as flavor.

TASTY GARNISHES: VEGETABLE VARIETY

Garnishes of the vegetable variety are made from ingredients that come off a tree, a bush, or a plant, or grow in the ground. Naturally, these offerings will be on the healthier side but, hopefully, just as tastily satisfying. Try the candied popcorn for your next binge-watch or just to satisfy your sweet + salty tooth next to an ice-cold glass of Oolong Cola (page 84). Or how about Walnut + Miso Butter (page 136) on crunchy seven-grain toast? It's the perfect sidekick to cocktail #24, Miso + Manuka Honey + Islay Whisky (page 210), or a straight shot of peaty Scotch whisky.

ALL DRIED OUT

One of my favorite kitchen gadgets is a dehydrator, which sort of looks like a small air-conditioning unit and, in fact, is quite similar in function in that it blows air (except the air is hot) and is meant to suck the moisture out of whatever you put into its chambers. It's used to create things such as jerky or fruit leather, or to dry herbs rapidly. In modernist kitchens, it's also used to dry crackers flat that are then deep-fried into puffed-up Doritos-style garnishes, except they're made with mushrooms or beets.

My reason for loving this contraption is that it helps me make dusts and dried chips that can be sprinkled on top of the drink for added flavor or served alongside as a snack. I make two types of dust—fruit or veggie based, or spirit and sugar based. Both are relatively simple to make; it just takes a bit of time and patience.

Dried chips are just a matter of slicing thinly enough so they dry rapidly. This can also be done with a Silpat nonstick baking mat in a super-low-temp oven. Dehydrators vary in price—I use one by Excalibur for commercial kitchens, but smaller models can be found online for as little as $40.

WHIPPED BROWN BUTTER

MAKES 1 CUP [224 G]

My favorite way to serve butter alongside a drink is to whip it and schmear it onto a nice skinny cracker. If you want to cut some of that fattiness, serve it with crunchy radishes or Pickled Kumquats (page 130).

2 sticks [224 g] unsalted butter
Salt of your choice

Cut both sticks of butter into ½-in [2.5-cm] slices. Place 1 stick in a small heatproof bowl and the other stick into a small saucepan.

Heat the butter in the pan over medium heat for 6 to 8 minutes until the solids start to caramelize and turn brown and the foam subsides.

This is your brown butter. Pour the brown butter over the butter in the heatproof bowl and stir briefly. Refrigerate and let cool.

Once cooled, transfer the butter to a food processor or a medium bowl. Add salt to taste. Process, or use a handheld mixer, to whip the butter until light and fluffy. This will keep, covered and refrigerated, for about 2 months.

WHIPPED LARDO

MAKES 2 CUPS [400 G]

In a mood for some savory decadence? Whip up a bowl of this luscious aromatic lardo, great slathered on toasted bread and paired with a simple Bourbon Old-Fashioned.

2 cups [400 g] ground pork fat (you can get this from any good butcher)
1 Tbsp kosher salt
½ tsp Himalayan pink salt
1 tsp fennel pollen
1 tsp freshly ground black pepper

In a medium bowl, combine the pork fat, kosher and pink salts, pollen, and pepper. Stir to incorporate the spices.

Cover the bowl with plastic wrap and refrigerate overnight (the salt will cure the fat).

Remove from the refrigerator and whip with a handheld electric mixer to aerate the pork fat and increase its volume slightly. Refrigerate in an airtight container until ready to use, up to 1 week.

WHIPPED HONEY BUTTER

MAKES ABOUT 1½ CUPS [191 G]

A decadent and fragrant spread to schmear on a cracker and serve alongside a glass of whisky, or dollop onto slices of apples or banana. For a switch, substitute ½ tsp ground cinnamon for the bee pollen.

1 stick [112 g] unsalted butter, at room temperature

3 Tbsp [65 g] Manuka or other runny honey

1 Tbsp [14 g] bee pollen or fennel pollen

In a small bowl, blend together the butter, honey, and pollen. Refrigerate in an airtight container until ready to use.

Transfer the butter to a food processor or a medium bowl. Process, or use a handheld mixer, to whip the butter until light and fluffy. This will keep, covered and refrigerated, for about 1 month.

WALNUT + MISO BUTTER

MAKES ABOUT 2½ CUPS [ABOUT 300 G]

I have an obsession with all things sweet and salty. This earthy nut butter is no exception and finds its way onto pretty much everything, including (but not limited to) cookies, ice cream, smoothies, toast, and crackers, or even just a cheeky spoonful on a sliced banana is enough of a fix for me.

½ lb [226 g] raw shelled walnut halves or pieces

¼ cup [60 ml] coconut nectar or date nectar

1 Tbsp [14 g] white miso

1 Tbsp [15 ml] water

½ tsp vanilla extract

1 tsp smoked salt

Preheat the oven to 275°F [135°C]. Line a baking sheet with parchment paper and sprinkle the nuts onto the parchment. Toast for 15 to 20 minutes.

Remove from the oven and let cool completely. Transfer the cooled nuts to a food processor and process into a paste.

Add the nectar, miso, water, vanilla, and salt. Continue blending until smooth. Transfer to an airtight container, where it will keep for about 1 week, if you can resist it that long.

NOTE: *Add date pieces and/or walnut bits for a chunkier texture.*

PARMESAN FRICOS

MAKES 6 TO 8 FRICOS, DEPENDING ON HOW THICK YOU LAYER THE CHEESE

Other than Prosciutto Chips (page 138), the only other type of animal chips I use for drink/sidekick garnishes are Parmesan Fricos, a fancy word for melted grated cheese. These fricos are delicious paired with veggie juice–based drinks, such as the #10 cocktail, Lettuce + Celery + Mezcal (page 178). Both types of chips are insanely easy to make. You will need access to an oven, however, and a cheese grater.

One 5-oz (142-g) hunk good-quality Parmesan cheese (cow's milk and nutty) or Pecorino Romano cheese (sheep's milk and salty), grated into a medium grate
Freshly ground black pepper
Zest of 1 lemon (optional)
Garlic powder for sprinkling

Preheat the oven to 400°F (200°C). Line a baking sheet with parchment paper.

In a large bowl, combine the grated cheese, pepper to taste, and lemon zest (if using).

Place a 2½-in [6-cm] round unfluted cookie cutter (or wing it and sprinkle the cheese into rustic random shapes) on the prepared sheet and sprinkle an even layer of cheese into the cutter. Sprinkle with garlic powder. Move the cutter and repeat until you've used up the remaining cheese, sprinkling each round with garlic powder.

Bake for 3 to 5 minutes. Remove from the oven and let cool. Use a flat spatula to transfer the melted chips to a plate to cool. Store in an airtight container at room temperature for about 1 week with a silica packet inside to absorb any moisture.

PROSCIUTTO CHIPS

MAKES 10 CHIPS

Crunchy, salty, intense umami-ness in every bite. Scatter these chips over a simple green salad or serve alongside a glass of dry vermouth or sherry. For a switch, dust with fennel pollen if you prefer.

10 prosciutto leaves, thinly sliced

Chinese five-spice powder (optional)

Preheat the oven to 375°F [190°C]. Line a baking sheet with parchment paper.

Lay the prosciutto leaves on the prepared sheet and dust with Chinese five-spice powder (if using). Bake for about 12 minutes until crispy.

Remove from the oven and let cool. Use a flat spatula to transfer the chips to a plate to cool completely. Keep refrigerated in an airtight container for about 1 week.

CANDIED OLIVES OR CRANBERRIES

MAKES ABOUT 1 CUP [140 G] OLIVES OR 1 CUP [100 G] CRANBERRIES

I created these candied olives a few years ago as another sweet-and-salty foil to a spritzy Highball inspired by one of my favorite Italian appetizers—simple sliced oranges with slivers of shaved fennel—accented with spicy Moroccan olives. Your olives should be pitted so there are no surprise crunches in your mouth. I prefer firm olives these days, such as Castelvetrano, but uber-salty and spicy dried black olives are just as fabulous.

The cranberries are a variation on the olive recipe. Use this super-tart fruit to accent a spiced apple cider or as a treat with sliced apples and cheeses.

1 cup [140 g] pitted Castelvetrano olives or [100 g] fresh cranberries
¼ cup [60 ml] fresh lemon juice
¼ cup [60 ml] water
¼ cup [50 g] plus 2 tsp cane sugar or coconut nectar, divided
1 tsp togarashi (optional)

Preheat the oven to 300°F [150°C]. Line a baking sheet with parchment paper and set aside.

In a heavy-bottomed saucepan set over medium heat, combine the olives, or cranberries, lemon juice, water, and ¼ cup [50 g] sugar. Bring to a boil, turn the heat to low, and simmer for 5 to 6 minutes, letting the liquid reduce to a thick syrup. It's ready when you can drag a spoon through the syrup and it leaves a trail behind; the thicker the syrup, the longer it takes for that trail to fill.

Spoon the olives, or cranberries, onto the prepared sheet, separating them so they don't touch. Bake for 15 to 20 minutes, checking that they're not burning.

Remove from the oven, transfer to a medium bowl, and sprinkle with the remaining 2 tsp sugar and togarashi (if using), making sure they are coated on all sides. Store in an airtight container at room temperature with a silica packet inside to absorb any moisture for up to 5 days. Do not refrigerate or they become too damp.

SESAME + CHINESE FIVE-SPICE CANDIED POPCORN

MAKES ABOUT 3 CUPS [24 G]

This popcorn is a bit of an out-of-the-box flavor combination inspired by my love of cold noodle salad. Try it—I predict it becomes a craveable addition to your snacktime arsenal.

¼ cup [60 ml] coconut nectar or date nectar

1 Tbsp [14 g] tahini

1 Tbsp [15 ml] water

½ tsp Chinese five-spice powder

½ tsp freshly ground black pepper

3 cups [24 g] freshly popped plain popcorn

1 tsp smoked salt

1 Tbsp [4 g] black sesame seeds

Preheat the oven to 300°F [150°C]. Line a baking sheet with parchment paper and set aside.

In a large bowl, mix together the nectar, tahini, water, five-spice powder, and pepper until they form a smooth syrup. Add the popcorn and stir to evenly coat. (Do not let the popcorn sit in the syrup for too long or it will deflate and lose its pop!) Transfer the popcorn to the prepared sheet, separating the kernels to keep them from clumping. Bake for 5 to 7 minutes.

Remove from the oven and sprinkle with the salt and sesame seeds. Let cool before eating. Store for a few hours only in an airtight container, but it generally doesn't last long enough to be stored!

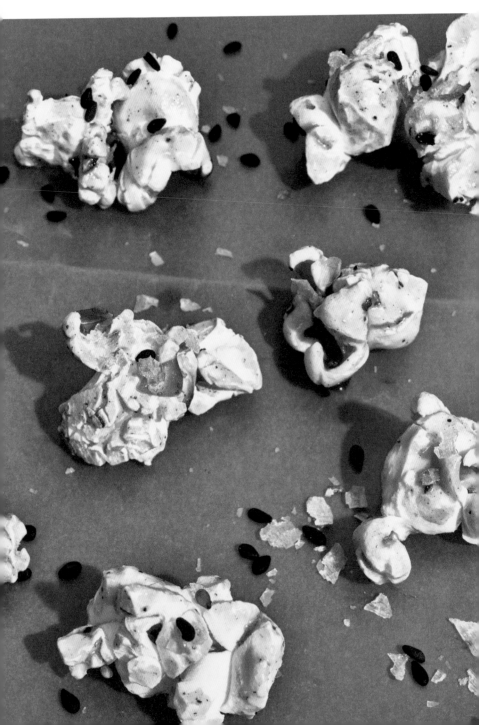

MISO-CANDIED WALNUTS
OR POPCORN

MAKES ABOUT 2½ CUPS [250 G] WALNUTS OR 2½ CUPS [20 G] POPCORN

Serve this tasty treat as a side snack with cocktails, or fill a party bowl and watch it disappear. We use the same ratio as the Walnut + Miso Butter (page 136) here, but instead of grinding the nuts or popcorn, they're tossed in the syrup and baked.

2½ cups [250 g] raw shelled walnut halves or 2½ cups [20 g] freshly popped plain popcorn

¼ cup [60 ml] coconut nectar or date nectar

1 Tbsp [14 g] white miso

1 Tbsp [15 ml] water

½ tsp vanilla extract

1 tsp smoked salt

Preheat the oven to 300°F [150°C]. Line a baking sheet with parchment paper and sprinkle the nuts onto the parchment. Toast for 15 to 20 minutes (you will know when they are done; your kitchen will fill up with their scented goodness).

Meanwhile, in a large bowl, mix together the nectar, miso, water, and vanilla. Once the nuts are toasted, or the popcorn is popped, toss it into the bowl and stir to coat with the miso syrup. Transfer the mixture back to the parchment-lined sheet and bake for 5 to 7 minutes longer.

Remove from the oven and sprinkle with the salt. Let cool before eating. These treats are best eaten the day they're made, but you can store them in an airtight container at room temperature for 1 day if needed . . . they just won't be as fresh.

FRUIT OR VEGETABLE CHIPS

YIELD VARIES BASED ON YOUR INGREDIENTS

Add a bit of crunch to your garnish game with a dried fruit or veggie chip. Turn the carrot strips into petrified curls or pop a delicate stained glass window–like orange slice jauntily on the side of your cocktail glass for an edible fascinator. I generally start with one or two large beets or apples, four carrots, one pineapple, or two or three firm tomatoes (see Note).

Gather together the following equipment to make this recipe: sharp mandoline slicer, dehydrator or a baking sheet, Silpat mat, and an oven.

Your choice: apples, pineapple, blood oranges, lemons, tomatoes, beets, or carrots, washed well and dried

If using a dehydrator, turn it to the highest temperature setting; if using an oven, preheat it to the lowest possible setting.

Line the dehydrator shelves with parchment paper and lightly spray them with vegetable oil. This prevents the dried slices from sticking and tearing when you peel them off. If using an oven, line a baking sheet with a Silpat mat.

Stand the mandoline slicer upright in a large bowl. Slice the fruit or vegetables downward to get a paper-thin [1-mm] slice, letting each fall into the bowl. When you have about 20 slices, place them on the parchment-lined shelves and into the dehydrator for about 8 hours (or the Silpat-lined baking sheet and into the oven for about 8 hours). If using an oven, pay closer attention to checking more frequently for doneness.

Check on the slices periodically. If you are in a humid climate, it can take a little longer to dry them out. You want crisp slices that still have flavor; what you don't want is half-dried and rubbery, or decimated and shriveled, slices.

When dried, carefully remove the slices from the parchment (or Silpat) so as not to tear them. Store in an airtight container at room temperature for a couple of months with 2 or 3 silica packets inside to absorb any moisture.

NOTE: *If drying tomatoes, remove the seeds and pat the slices dry on clean kitchen towels before you dehydrate. Also, tomatoes can take longer, up to 3 days, because of their water content. In general, don't dehydrate ingredients with a high water content—though it will work, it will waste a whole lot of energy getting there.*

CAMPARI OR FERNET DUST

MAKES ABOUT 1 CUP [120 G]

As simple as this recipe is, it took me a few months of trial and error to figure out how to get this bittersweet powder not to clump. My early mistake was using cane sugar. Once I cottoned on that to get a powdery dust I needed to start with powder as my base, I was off to the races. The key ingredient to achieving this texture is the cornstarch that forms the base of powdered sugar. I use this dust as a playful garnish to add texture or a new level of flavor to my cocktails. And because the alcohol burns off in the cooking process (though the sugar does not), you can use this in both Clean and Dirty drinks.

Gather together a dehydrator, small Silpat mat, and a coffee or spice grinder for this recipe. Make sure the grinder has been cleaned and dried—if it smells like coffee or spices, take the time to remove those aromas before grinding.

1 cup [240 ml] Campari or Fernet
1 cup [120 g] powdered sugar (this has to be powdered sugar because the cornstarch in it helps create the dust texture)

Turn the dehydrator to the highest temperature setting and place the Silpat mat on the dehydrator sheet. Set aside.

In a medium bowl, stir together the liqueur and sugar until all the lumps have dissolved. Alternatively, use a fine-mesh strainer to sift the powdered sugar into the liquid. Pour the sugar mixture into a heavy-bottomed saucepan over medium heat. Heat until the mixture starts to bubble and reduce, stirring every few seconds to make sure it's not burning. Once the mixture starts to resemble a rather thick glue-like consistency, 8 to 10 minutes, remove it from the heat and let it cool slightly.

Carefully spread the cooled mixture onto the Silpat mat, making sure it's as even as possible and not running over the sides. (If it's too runny, transfer the mixture in a bowl to an ice bath to firm up a wee bit before spreading onto the Silpat.) Place the Silpat-lined tray into the dehydrator and let dry for at least 12 hours. It's ready when the sugar syrup starts to crack.

Scrape off the dried sugar mix and transfer it to your clean grinder chamber. Attach the lid and grind it to a fine powder. Store in an airtight container at room temperature for 2 to 3 months with a couple of silica packets inside to help keep the dust from clumping. The bitter flavor will begin to diminish if it's kept too long.

NOTE: *Because this is cooked, most of the alcohol burns off, so it's important that the liqueur you choose has a strong* flavor. That way, you will still taste it after the spirit portion evaporates (in other words, there's no point in making powdered vodka—it has no taste, so you'll just be left with powdered sugar).

remove those aromas before grinding. The yield varies depending on the size of your veggie chips. You'll need 10 to 20 dehydrated Fruit or Vegetable Chips (page 143).

VARIATION:
FRUIT OR VEGETABLE DUST

You'll need a coffee or spice grinder for this recipe. Make sure it has been cleaned and dried—if it smells like coffee or spices, take the time to

Place the dried chips into the grinding chamber of your clean coffee or spice grinder. Secure the lid and pulse until your chips turn into a medium-fine powder. Store in an airtight container at room temperature for a couple of months with 2 or 3 silica packets inside to keep the powder from clumping.

AIR HEADS

Airs and foams play a major role in most modernist cook's dishes. They offer a way to add subtle flavor and a new texture to a plate. For a while, I added a foam to pretty much half the drinks I made—for me it lends another visually playful element and is a chance to bring in additional scent or flavor at the beginning of the tasting experience. For instance, a salt foam on top of a glass of grapefruit juice instantly elevates this simple beverage to another level, or add a spicy beer foam to a classic Michelada (beer, hot sauce, and citrus).

What's the difference between an air and a foam, I hear you ask. They are both made from a liquid that contains a form of stabilizer to help the air or foam stay fluffy, but here the similarity ends.

AIRS

An air is usually a liquid that has a stabilizer added and has been agitated with a handheld blender or whisk. The bubbles tend to be bigger than a foam, but you can also aerate a foam with the help of a fish pump (a clean one!).

FOAMS

Foams tend to be denser or thicker than airs (the bubbles tend to be smaller and tightly packed), but not so thick that you can't drink through it. Foams are generally, but not always, whipped using an iSi gun or cream whipper to achieve their texture. Instead of air, they are inflated with N_2O, nitrous oxide gas—the gas inside a Reddi-wip canister. Most foams here contain either a fat-based substance or an emulsifier, which have molecules that, when charged with gas, form bonds with each other to hold a foam. Because of this, no modernist "voodoo" powder is needed.

To keep things simple, for all the foam recipes, gather together an iSi cream whipper gadget and one or two N_2O gas cartridges. This method is used for all foam recipes here as well:

Add all your ingredients to the iSi chamber and secure the lid. Shake to incorporate everything.

Charge once with N_2O gas and shake vigorously to distribute the gas. Test by squirting a small amount into a glass. If it is still a bit runny, charge it a second time (two charges should be plenty).

To use, invert the iSi whipper and dispense about 1 heaping tablespoon [about 15 g] of foam on top of your drink—don't go over the rim, however. Once the foam loses its charge, it will start to run down your pretty glass and create a mess. This keeps for 2 to 3 days, refrigerated. It will need to be recharged after 12 hours.

NOTE: *Chill your mixture, which may eliminate the need to charge it twice. Keep it refrigerated between uses.*

LEMON VERBENA AIR

MAKES ABOUT 16 CUPS [4 L], WHEN AERATED

Spoon over a glass of champagne or gussy up an iced tea with an aromatic delicateness.

Gather together an immersion or handheld electric blender and a gram scale for this recipe.

¼ cup [60 ml] warm water or Riesling
¼ cup [60 ml] Lemon Verbena Syrup (see Lemon Thyme Syrup, page 77)
1 Tbsp [15 ml] white balsamic vinegar
1½ tsp vanilla extract
1½ tsp Texturas Sucro (see Resources, page 211)

In a small bowl or pitcher, combine the water, syrup, vinegar, vanilla, and Texturas Sucro. Use an immersion (or handheld) blender to blend everything until bubbles form.

To use, with a slotted spoon or Julep strainer, carefully spoon out 1 to 2 Tbsp [15 to 30 ml], depending on the size of your glass, and place it on top of your drink. This keeps for 2 days, refrigerated. You will need to reaerate it because the air bubbles will subside.

NOTE: *This recipe works with any of the compound syrups (see pages 70 to 77).*

CLEAN SALTY DOG AIR

MAKES ABOUT 16 CUPS [4 L], WHEN AERATED

This offers a fun way to add a savory component to #1 Grapefruit + Hops + Gin (page 157), or use to top a Margarita or grapefruit soda. It's based on the classic Salty Dog cocktail that has a salt rim. Instead, though, this rich smoked salt is dissolved and incorporated into a grapefruit and lime solution laced with a naturally derived emulsifier that helps whip the whole shebang into a light and airy frenzy.

You'll need an immersion or handheld blender for this recipe.

¼ cup [60 ml] warm water

¼ cup [60 ml] fresh grapefruit juice

1 Tbsp [15 ml] fresh lime juice

1½ tsp Maldon smoked sea salt flakes

1½ tsp Texturas Sucro (see Resources, page 211)

In a small bowl or pitcher, combine the water, grapefruit and lime juices, salt, and Texturas Sucro. Use an immersion (or handheld) blender to blend everything until bubbles form.

To use, with a slotted spoon or Julep strainer, carefully spoon out 1 to 2 Tbsp [15 to 30 ml], depending on the size of your glass, and place it on top of your drink. This keeps for 2 days, refrigerated. You will need to reaerate it because the air bubbles will subside.

VARIATION:
DIRTY SALTY DOG AIR

For a Dirty version, add ¼ cup [60 ml] elderflower liqueur.

NOTE: *I recently started using a small pump called the Magic Air Maker made by the folks at Modernist Pantry. You plug it in and air courses through the tubing that's placed in the solution, creating effortless bubbles.*

COCONUT-SPICED FOAM

MAKES ENOUGH TO GARNISH ABOUT 25 DRINKS

For a hint of coconut, use this foam on any tropical drink, or on iced coffee or as an alternative to whipped cream. Use the equipment and method described on page 146.

1½ cups [360 ml] full-fat coconut milk
¼ cup [60 ml] fresh lime juice
1½ tsp vanilla extract

½ cup plus 2 Tbsp [150 ml] Clean or Dirty Falernum (see Brown Rice Orgeat Variation: Falernum, page 81) or Cinnamon Syrup (see Spiced Simple Syrup, page 69)

IPA BEER OR HOPS SYRUP FOAM

MAKES ENOUGH TO GARNISH ABOUT 25 DRINKS

This is great to top off any bitter aperitif, any grapefruit-based drink, or plain old lemonade. Use the equipment and method described on page 146.

1 cup [240 ml] IPA beer or ½ cup [120 ml] Hops Syrup (page 76) plus ½ cup [120 ml] water for a Clean version
1 cup [60 ml] fresh grapefruit juice
¼ cup [60 ml] elderflower liqueur (optional)

¼ cup [60 ml] aquafaba (see page 118) or egg white
2 Tbsp [30 ml] salt solution (10 parts water to 1 part salt)

SPICED APPLE CIDER FOAM

Use this foam to top a glass of apple cider, mulled wine, or a classic Sazerac cocktail. Use the equipment and method described on page 146.

1½ cups [360 ml] fresh-pressed apple cider

2 Tbsp [30 ml] fresh lemon juice

½ cup [120 ml] Clean or Dirty Spiced Simple Syrup (page 69; mulling spice, allspice, Chinese five-spice powder, or cinnamon all work)

¼ cup [60 ml] aquafaba (see page 118) or egg white

1½ tsp vanilla extract

Pinch of salt

BEET KOMBUCHA FOAM

MAKES ENOUGH TO GARNISH ABOUT 25 DRINKS

This adds an earthy finish to a Negroni, a Shandy, or a simple ginger beer. Use the equipment and method described on page 146.

1 cup [240 ml] Ginger + Manuka Kombucha (page 116)

½ cup [120 ml] fresh beet juice

¼ cup [60 ml] Clean or Dirty Ginger Syrup (page 89) or Raw Honey Syrup (page 70)

¼ cup [60 ml] aquafaba (see page 118) or egg white (for stabilizer)

1½ tsp vanilla extract

Pinch of salt

CHAPTER THREE:
CLEAN+DIRTY
COCKTAILS

Congratulations! You made it this far, hopefully with some happy hours spent stirring syrups, distilling home-made infusions, exploring the flavorful art of creative garnishes, perhaps fomenting a foam or two. Now it's time to put all the intelligence you gleaned from chapters one and two into practice and actually start crafting some cocktails.

Instead of clever names, the 24 recipes in the following pages are simply numbered and described by the trio (and sometimes quartet) of main flavor notes. They are organized by season, celebrating the produce, pastimes, and spirit of each. And in the spirits department, you'll see I developed both a spiked, or "Dirty," and a "Clean" version of every recipe. The Clean recipes swap in alcohol-free bases, equally up to the task of sup-porting the structure of the drink; they do not want for flavor, of course, built upon the same principles of depth, balance, and use of fresh and interesting, complemen-tary ingredients. They also adhere to other rules of clean eating, such as avoiding refined sugars. The Dirty recipes, while ranging from boozy to lightly alcoholic, share with the Clean versions the incorporation of ingredients with powerful health benefits, from a blast of vitamin C and its antioxidants to inflammation- and cholesterol-fighting superfoods.

I emphasize again, it's crucial to the success of these drinks to follow the recipes closely for proportion and technique. You can certainly substitute ingredients as inspiration, or necessity, strikes. If you can't find kumquats, grapefruit can work fine; you might imagine cilantro will be better than parsley in a mix; or you may be more in a brandy mood than a bourbon state of mind. Follow your hunches and go for it. Making drinks should be fun—like a musician with a guitar, you should be open to improvisation and riffing. Who knows what beautiful melodies will emerge?

SPRING

As a kid growing up in a fairly rural part of the English Midlands, I was accustomed to the first signs of spring thaw coming a little later than in the southern counties. The frozen earth began to warm slowly sometime in March or later, but ah, you knew when spring was coming: The fragile white crystals on the grass melting into morning dew, and my Gramps Joe picking up his hustle were the biggest signals. Gramps would start disappearing more and more often into his little patch of heaven, taking stock of Jack Frost's damage to his bean shed or the cold frame. I'd wait in anticipatory agony for the first tender green shoots to poke through the loamy earth, praying a surprise cold snap wouldn't knock them out before they got their chance to blossom into paper whites, daffodils, and bluebells. When those early bloomers exploded forth, I'd gather big bouquets to fill my room with their heady aromas. There's nothing like gulping in the perfume of spring's first flowers to clear winter out of one's brain.

And then there were the geese. Now, as then, hearing their calls to each other as they gracefully pass overhead on their return journey brings a visceral reaction, a tear to my eye, and a sigh of thanks for the cycle of rebirth—of my garden, of the planet, and of hope. There's also a huge part of me that's jealous of those birds and their wandering ways; I wish I could fly with them, like them, so far and with so many adventures, I imagine, and then return home to new beginnings and to family.

Spring here in Southern California is far more predictable, but no less inspiring or bountiful. The first signs of it at the market are fragrant, rose-hued stems of rhubarb; plump kumquats; and peppery, saffron-colored nasturtiums. These are the stunning gifts I've dreamed about all winter, arriving to add vibrancy and special magic to my liquid offerings—perfect mates for lighter, unaged elixirs, such as botanical gin, *eaux de vie*, grassy *rhum agricole*, refreshing fruit ales and aperitif wines, or simple citrus spritzers. Cheers to the rebirth of all this edible life!

GRAPEFRUIT + HOPS + GIN

MAKES 1 CLEAN OR DIRTY COCKTAIL

While I am an ardent fan of all five "basic tastes," I really love bitter. This drink vision came to me a few years ago, when I added bitters and sugar to a fruity, hoppy IPA. The beer was mildly entertaining on its own, but these additions plus a splash of grapefruit juice transformed it into a refreshing, early evening fizz. Just like the Count with his Negroni (see page 160), I added gin for a bigger kick. The lovely elderflower liqueur, called St-Germain, complements the hops. For a finishing touch, dress it up with a lick of smoked salt and a dollop of salty foam; these invite every taste bud to the party.

With the Dirty version, you have the choice of just dipping your toes in with a low-ABV Shandy-style drink or go all the way in with gin.

CLEAN

Black salt or smoked salt, for the rim

1 lemon wedge

¼ cup plus 2 Tbsp [90 ml] fresh grapefruit juice

1 Tbsp [45 ml] Clean Hops Syrup (page 76)

1 Tbsp [15 ml] fresh yuzu juice or fresh lime juice

¼ tsp alcohol-free vanilla extract

2 or 3 drops alcohol-free gentian root tincture (see Note, page 161)

Ice cubes for shaking

Soda or sparkling water, chilled (see Note)

Clean Salty Dog Air (page 148) for garnish

Rim a coupe or Martini glass with salt: Pour a layer of salt into a small, shallow dish. Rub the lemon wedge around the rim of the glass and dip the rim into the salt until evenly coated. Tap the glass gently to remove any loose grains and set aside.

In a cocktail shaker, combine the grapefruit juice, syrup, yuzu juice, vanilla, and gentian root tincture. Add 5 ice cubes, cover the shaker, and shake for about 3 seconds.

Using a Hawthorne strainer, strain the drink into the salt-rimmed glass. Top with a splash of soda water. Spoon 1 to 2 Tbsp [15 to 30 ml] salty air over the top and serve immediately. Drink without a straw to get all the flavors of the drink and its salty accompaniments.

NOTE: *The Clean version of this drink lends itself to a Perlini shaker, a nifty gadget that uses a pressurizer to carbonate your cocktails more than a splash of soda will. Here it adds an extra frisson to the bubbles, more like the action of the beer in the Dirty version. When using a Perlini, shake the mixture a little longer, about 5 seconds.*

Continued

DIRTY

Black salt or smoked salt, for the rim

1 lemon wedge

3 Tbsp [45 ml] dry gin, such as Beefeater
or Fords

3 Tbsp [45 ml] fresh grapefruit juice

2 Tbsp [30 ml] Clean or Dirty Hops Syrup
(page 76)

1 Tbsp [15 ml] St-Germain or other
elderflower liqueur

1 Tbsp [15 ml] fresh yuzu juice or fresh
lime juice

2 or 3 drops gentian root tincture
(see Note, page 161)

Ice cubes for shaking

2 Tbsp [30 ml] cold IPA beer

Clean or Dirty Salty Dog Air (page 148)
for garnish

Rim a coupe or Martini glass with
salt: Pour a layer of salt into a small,
shallow dish. Rub the lemon wedge
around the rim of the glass and
dip the rim into the salt until evenly
coated. Tap the glass gently to remove
any loose grains and set aside.

In a cocktail shaker, combine the
gin, grapefruit juice, syrup, St-Germain,
yuzu juice, and gentian root tincture.
Add 5 ice cubes, cover the shaker,
and shake hard for about 3 seconds.

Using a Hawthorne strainer,
strain the drink into the salt-rimmed
glass. Top with the beer. Spoon 1 to
2 Tbsp [15 to 30 ml] salty air over the
top and serve immediately. Drink without a straw to get all the flavors of the
drink and its salty accompaniments.

VARIATION:
GRAPEFRUIT SHANDY

For a hoppy (and less alcoholic)
Grapefruit Shandy, omit the gin
and increase the beer to ¼ cup plus
1 Tbsp [75 ml].

#2

KUMQUAT + CORIANDER + "CAMPARI" + MEZCAL

MAKES 1 CLEAN OR DIRTY COCKTAIL

Ask any seasoned bartender what her favorite off-shift drink is and many will name the Negroni. Legend has it that a bartender in Florence, Italy, created this drink for Count Negroni when he requested a stiffer version of his usual Americano—a mix of bitter Campari liqueur and sweet vermouth topped with soda water. In the Negroni, the soda water is replaced with gin and the lemon twist with an orange twist. Because this drink's popularity has only increased over the hundred or so years since its legendary creation, clearly the Count wasn't the only one blown away.

While the Negroni is indeed one of my go-to sips, the traditional recipe was begging to be cleaned up. Both the Clean and Dirty versions here are less sweet than the Negroni. In the Dirty recipe, I switched out the gin for nuanced mezcal made from wild, foraged agave hearts smoked in giant fire pits before distillation. Also in the Dirty rendition, you have the option of using trademarked Campari—originally made to help digestion—but I encourage you to eschew the artificial color and make my proprietary hippie "Campari" bitters (page 96), which you need for the Clean version. Any option delivers the coriander note in this heady herb-driven drink.

Verjus, translates to green juice—in other words, unripe juice—and comes in two colors (red and white . . . *ver* actually stands for "unripe," not green here). It is used in dressings, mostly, and to add delicate acidulation to recipes such as the one that follows. It is a liquid that I use as a stand-in for citrus when I want the resulting cocktail to be transparent.

CLEAN

3 kumquats, halved through the equator

¼ cup plus 1 Tbsp [75 ml] Clean "Campari" Bitters (page 96)

2 Tbsp [30 ml] white *verjus*

1 Tbsp [15 ml] Clean Basic Simple Syrup (page 69)

2 or 3 drops alcohol-free gentian root tincture (see Note)

Ice cubes for stirring

1 rock ice cube for serving

Orange twist for garnish

Soda or sparkling water, chilled (optional)

In a short rocks glass, lightly muddle the kumquats. Set aside.

In a mixing glass, combine the bitters, *verjus*, simple syrup, and gentian root tincture. Add 6 ice cubes and stir with a long-handled mixing spoon for about 5 seconds.

Add the rock cube to the glass with the kumquats. Using a Hawthorne strainer, strain the drink into the glass. Squeeze the orange peel over the drink to release the oils. Rub the peel around the rim of the glass and drop it in. Top with a splash of soda water, if you like.

NOTE: *Gentian is a bitter herb used for hundreds of years by herbalists, mainly for liver and kidney health and to treat gastrointestinal imbalances. It adds a distinct extra bitter note to the herbal profile of this drink. Start with 2 drops when first making this drink to see how bitter you want it. You'll find both regular and alcohol-free tinctures at well-stocked natural foods stores.*

DIRTY

3 kumquats, halved through the equator

¼ cup [60 ml] Dirty "Campari" Bitters (page 97)

2 Tbsp [30 ml] sweet vermouth

2 Tbsp [30 ml] mezcal

2 or 3 drops gentian root tincture (see Note)

Ice cubes for stirring

1 rock ice cube for serving

Orange twist for garnish

Soda water or prosecco, chilled (optional)

In a short rocks glass, lightly muddle the kumquats. Set aside.

In a mixing glass, combine the bitters, vermouth, mezcal, and gentian root tincture. Add 6 ice cubes and stir with a long-handled mixing spoon for about 5 seconds.

Add the rock cube to the glass with the kumquats. Using a Hawthorne strainer, strain the drink into the glass. Squeeze the orange peel over the drink to release the oils. Rub the peel around the rim of the glass and drop it in. Top with a splash of soda water or prosecco, if you like.

#3

NASTURTIUM + PEAS + RHUM AGRICOLE

MAKES 1 CLEAN OR DIRTY COCKTAIL

As a fledgling drink maker, I must have made thousands of rummy Mojitos—about a thousand every weekend, it seems like, in the upscale Mexican restaurant where I worked in the heart of New York City's Chelsea neighborhood. I wondered many times why, apparently, no one had switched out the mint. Experimenting with all potential variations using other gorgeous, fragrant herbs or a selection of botanicals, I finally landed on this combination, my favorite by a mile. Nasturtiums and pea shoots mingle to make a drink that is at once grassy, fragrant, and spicy as well as delightfully refreshing.

Nasturtiums, those bright-yellow blossoms tumbling out of many a garden bed on long, leafy vines, have edible flowers packed full of vitamin C. They grow fairly easily in window boxes as well, with enough water and a drink of fertilizer once a week; you'll also find them at farmers' markets. Try adding the pretty petals to salads, where they are gorgeously eye-catching until you bite into their surprising peppery kick. Look for pea tendrils at your local farmers' market or specialty grocer.

CLEAN

4 English pea shoots (tendrils)

3 Tbsp [45 ml] fresh lime juice

3 Tbsp [45 ml] Clean Basic Simple Syrup (page 69)

6 or 7 fresh nasturtium flower heads

5 large fresh mint leaves

2 or 3 drops alcohol-free gentian root tincture (see Note, page 161)

Ice cubes for shaking and serving

Splash of soda or sparkling water, chilled (optional)

In a cocktail shaker, combine 3 pea shoots with the lime juice and syrup. Muddle lightly.

Add 5 nasturtiums, the mint, gentian root tincture, and 5 ice cubes. Cover the shaker and shake hard for about 5 seconds; the ice will do the job of macerating the mint and flower petals into the drink.

Using a Hawthorne strainer, strain the shaker's contents into a chilled wineglass. Add more ice, if needed, to fill the glass, and top with a splash of soda water, if you like. Garnish with a pea shoot and a nasturtium flower or two.

DIRTY

4 English pea shoots

¼ cup [60 ml] *rhum agricole* or white rum

2 Tbsp [30 ml] fresh lime juice

2 Tbsp [30 ml] Clean or Dirty Basic
Simple Syrup (page 69)

6 or 7 fresh nasturtium flower heads

5 large fresh mint leaves

2 or 3 drops gentian root tincture (see
Note, page 161)

Ice cubes for shaking and serving

Splash of soda or sparkling water, chilled
(optional)

In a cocktail shaker, combine 3 pea
shoots, the rum, lime juice, and syrup.
Muddle lightly.

Add 5 nasturtiums, the mint,
gentian root tincture, and 5 ice
cubes. Cover the shaker and shake
hard for about 5 seconds; the ice will
do the job of macerating the mint and
flower petals into the drink.

Using a Hawthorne strainer,
strain the shaker's contents into a
chilled wineglass. Add more ice, if
needed, to fill the glass, and top with
a splash of soda water, if you like.
Garnish with a pea shoot and a nasturtium flower or two.

#4

PARSLEY + KEY LIME + VODKA

MAKES 1 CLEAN OR DIRTY COCKTAIL

Parsley is getting more renown for its superfood qualities. It contains masses of vitamins K and C, as well as folic acid, flavonoids, and antioxidants. It also contains a good amount of calcium, a plus for aging bones. From the drink maker's standpoint, its bright herbal flavor tastes a lot like citrus zest. For a low-ABV version of the Dirty recipe, omit the vodka and double up on the parsley-infused vermouth.

CLEAN

3 Tbsp [45 ml] fresh Key lime juice or fresh lime juice

3 Tbsp [45 ml] Key Lime Syrup (page 92)

2 Tbsp [30 ml] fresh parsley juice

2 Tbsp [30 ml] aquafaba (see page 118)

¼ tsp alcohol-free pure vanilla extract

2 or 3 drops alcohol-free gentian root tincture (see Note, page 161)

Ice cubes for shaking

Large fresh parsley leaf for garnish

In a cocktail shaker, combine the lime juice, syrup, parsley juice, aquafaba, vanilla, and gentian root tincture. Add 1 small piece of ice, cover the shaker, and whip shake for 5 seconds until you can no longer hear the ice rattling in the shaker.

Add 3 more ice cubes, cover the shaker, and shake hard for about 5 seconds more to chill. Using a Hawthorne strainer, immediately strain the drink into a chilled coupe or Martini glass. Garnish with the parsley leaf.

DIRTY

3 Tbsp [45 ml] Key Lime Vodka (page 92)

3 Tbsp [45 ml] Parsley Vermouth (page 87)

2 Tbsp [30 ml] aquafaba (see page 118) or 1 egg white

1½ Tbsp [22 ml] fresh Key lime juice or fresh lime juice

1 Tbsp [15 ml] Clean or Dirty Basic Simple Syrup (page 69)

¼ tsp pure vanilla extract

2 or 3 drops gentian root tincture (see Note, page 161)

Ice cubes for shaking

Large fresh parsley leaf for garnish

In a cocktail shaker, combine the vodka, vermouth, aquafaba, lime juice, syrup, vanilla, and gentian root tincture. Add 1 small piece of ice, cover the shaker, and whip shake for 5 seconds until you can no longer hear ice rattling in the shaker.

Add 3 more ice cubes, cover the shaker, and shake hard for about 5 seconds more. Using a Hawthorne strainer, immediately strain the drink into a chilled coupe or Martini glass. Garnish with the parsley leaf.

5

RHUBARB + COCONUT + GIN

MAKES 1 CLEAN OR DIRTY COCKTAIL

In the UK, a common dessert at school was a slop of stewed rhubarb disguised (barely, by our lunch ladies) with an even nastier and lumpier fake custard. When I think of that dish now, I think, *poor rhubarb!* It spent so much precious energy combining sun and water and oxygen and nutrients to come to life, only to be annihilated by bad cooks for the supposed benefit of six-year-olds. Why *rhubarb??*

In defense of this particular school lunch, it could be noted that rhubarb is high in fiber and protein as well as a number of vitamins that help young bodies grow. The question then is: How do you prepare it so it is not just palatable but mouthwateringly alluring for all of us—little and big kids alike? I urge you to read on: Here are two beautiful rhubarb brews, a Clean spring fling and a Dirty rosy version of a Ramos Fizz.

CLEAN

¼ cup [60 ml] Rhubarb Consommé (page 62)

2 Tbsp [30 ml] coconut milk

2 Tbsp [30 ml] fresh lemon juice

2 Tbsp [30 ml] aquafaba (see page 118)

1 Tbsp [15 ml] Clean Basic Simple Syrup (page 69)

½ tsp rose water (I use Sadaf or Al Wahdi brands; see Resources, page 211)

Ice cubes for shaking

Soda water, chilled

1 long strip or a few spirals of lemon zest, or, if available, 1 edible rosebud for garnish

In a cocktail shaker, combine the consommé, coconut milk, lemon juice, aquafaba, syrup, and rose water. Add 1 small piece of ice, cover the shaker, and whip shake until you can barely hear the ice rattling, about 5 seconds until chilled and diluted to perfection.

Add 3 more ice cubes, cover the shaker, and shake hard for 5 seconds more. Using a Hawthorne strainer, immediately strain the drink into a chilled highball glass or stemless wineglass. Top with a splash of soda water and garnish with the lemon zest or rosebud.

Continued

DIRTY

3 Tbsp [45 ml] gin or strawberry-infused
   gin, when strawberries are in season
   (see "Infusions," page 86)

3 Tbsp [45 ml] Rhubarb Consommé
   (page 62)

2 Tbsp [30 ml] coconut milk

2 Tbsp [30 ml] fresh lemon juice

2 Tbsp [30 ml] aquafaba (see page 118)
   or 1 egg white

1 Tbsp [15 ml] Dirty or Clean Basic Simple
   Syrup (page 69)

½ tsp rose water (I use Sadaf or Al Wahdi
   brands; see Resources, page 211)

Ice cubes for shaking

Soda water, chilled

1 long strip or a few spirals of lemon zest
   or, if available, 1 edible rosebud for
   garnish

In a cocktail shaker, combine the gin, consommé, coconut milk, lemon juice, aquafaba, syrup, and rose water. Add 1 small piece of ice, cover the shaker, and whip shake until you can barely hear the ice rattling, about 5 seconds until chilled and diluted to perfection.

Add 3 more ice cubes, cover the shaker, and shake hard for 5 seconds more. Using a Hawthorne strainer, immediately strain the drink into a chilled highball glass or stemless wineglass. Top with a splash of soda water and garnish with the lemon zest or rosebud.

6

ROSE GERANIUM + RHUBARB + "PIMM'S"

MAKES 1 CLEAN OR DIRTY COCKTAIL

I can grow plants in abundance year-round to produce my own restorative, healing, and delicious botanicals. A particular favorite of mine are geraniums, an assortment that grows like weeds—and I'm especially in love, love, love with rose geraniums. Their scent is both intoxicating and invigorating at the same time—and on top of their olfactory profligacy, they also relieve stress, balance hormones, reduce depression, and alleviate the effects of menopause. No wonder I'm addicted! I use the leaves for infusing, and both leaves and flowers for garnishes.

This drink takes its cues from a classic Pimm's cup—a float of light, refreshing lambic ale or kombucha gives it a spritz.

CLEAN

¼ cup plus 2 Tbsp [90 ml] Clean Rhubarb "Pimm's" (page 95)

2 Tbsp [30 ml] fresh lemon juice

2 Tbsp [30 ml] Clean Basic Simple Syrup (page 69)

2 or 3 drops alcohol-free gentian root tincture (see Note, page 161)

Ice cubes for shaking

2 ripe strawberries, hulled and thinly sliced lengthwise

3 thin slices cucumber

Strawberry kombucha, chilled

Rose geranium leaf for garnish

In a cocktail shaker, combine the "Pimm's," lemon juice, syrup, and gentian root tincture.

Add 5 ice cubes, cover the shaker, and shake hard for 3 seconds.

Pour the shaker's contents into a stemless wineglass. Drop in the strawberry and cucumber slices, top with a splash of kombucha, and garnish with the rose geranium leaf.

DIRTY

¼ cup plus 2 Tbsp [90 ml] Dirty Rhubarb "Pimm's" (page 95)

2 Tbsp [30 ml] fresh lemon juice

2 Tbsp [30 ml] Clean or Dirty Basic Simple Syrup (page 69)

2 or 3 drops gentian root tincture (see Note, page 161)

Ice cubes for shaking

2 ripe strawberries, hulled and thinly sliced lengthwise

3 thin slices cucumber

Strawberry lambic ale or pilsner, chilled

Rose geranium leaf for garnish

In a cocktail shaker, combine the "Pimm's," lemon juice, syrup, and gentian root tincture.

Add 5 ice cubes, cover the shaker, and shake hard for 3 seconds.

Pour the shaker's contents into a stemless wineglass. Drop in the strawberry and cucumber slices, top with a splash of beer, and garnish with the rose geranium leaf.

SUMMER

Back home, when I was a kid, summer truly started with school holidays—and tennis. To be exact: Wimbledon, that bastion of English tradition that arrives alongside the first crops of strawberries, ripe and ready to be doused with cream, and crisp cucumber sandwiches, all washed down with cold glasses of bitter lemon or ginger beer.

Years later, all grown up and far away across the ocean here in Los Angeles, I still feel a rush of seasonal abandon come summer. With mountainous truckloads of fresh produce pouring in, that urge to skip meals in the heat of the season morphs slightly—veggie juices and cleanses become the norm for many, and it's not uncommon for an all-liquid diet to last for weeks at a time, as the opportunity for pouring on the health benefits of fresh, raw fruits and veggies plays in center court.

During these bountiful days, the farmers' markets here turn into an almost obscene botanical treasure hunt. The juiciest peaches and darkest Black Republican cherries literally vanish in seconds. Elbows and strollers become powerful weapons in the contest to be the most victorious plunderer.

One of the most exciting features of the market for me during these peak days is the abundance of every kind of leafy, aromatic, flavorful, and almost magically nutritional herb. My basket fills with lush specimens, such as holy basil, bergamot mint, and lemon verbena. Even in California, the fresh herbs at the supermarket during the rest of the year have nothing on the flavor, potent scent, and sheer variety of the summer herb season.

This section collects half a dozen recipes that celebrate super-summery tastes centered on herbs, including one unique lemony Caesar salad–centric sip and, of course, *de rigueur* summer strawberries. If only I'd understood the concept and value—and simple deliciousness—of a clean diet when I was a youngster, the practice of "eating your vegetables" might have fortified me more while I was a serial adventure-seeking runaway . . . but, as we all come to learn, what's important is the journey itself.

7

WATERMELON + BERGAMOT MINT + BOURBON

MAKES 1 CLEAN OR DIRTY COCKTAIL

A bracing mixture of sugar, bourbon, and fresh mint, Juleps have long been a beloved tradition at the Kentucky Derby, and their popularity has resurged recently in the era of neo-cocktail culture. The Julep is a rendition of a Middle Eastern drink called a *jalab*, which is a similar combination of aromatics mixed with sugar, water, or tea and served over shaved ice to put out the fire of the midday heat.

This is my spin on the Julep, a definitively summer mix made with sweet ripe watermelon juice and tomato consommé, as well as a healthy dose of stimulating garden herbs. Famously hydrating, watermelon is also rich in antioxidants, effective in lowering blood pressure, and helpful for maintaining a healthy digestive tract. If you live close to a good farmers' market and you like going big on presentation, look for mini watermelons. Scoop out the flesh to juice and use the shell in place of a Julep cup.

CLEAN

5 large fresh Thai or sweet basil leaves

Watermelon, Mint + Basil Mini Ice Cubes (page 30), made with bergamot mint, or crushed ice for serving

¼ cup plus 1 Tbsp [75 ml] watermelon + bergamot mint juice (see Note, page 172)

3 Tbsp [45 ml] Tomato Consommé (page 60)

1½ Tbsp [22 ml] fresh lemon juice

1 Tbsp [15 ml] Clean Basic Simple Syrup (page 69)

½ Tbsp [7.5 ml] rose water (I use Sadaf or Al Wahdi brands; see Resources, page 211)

2 or 3 drops alcohol-free gentian root tincture (see Note, page 161)

Small basil and mint sprigs and/or 1 edible pink rosebud for garnish

Powdered sugar for dusting (optional)

Put the basil leaves in the bottom of a Julep cup or stemless wineglass. Fill the cup with the mini ice cubes or crushed ice. Pour the watermelon + bergamot mint juice, consommé, lemon juice, syrup, rose water, and gentian root tincture over the ice. Insert a swizzle stick. Position your palms flat on either side of the swizzle stick and run your hands back and forth to spin and twirl the stick and stir the mixture.

Garnish with the herb sprigs and/or rosebud, dust with powdered sugar, if you like, and serve immediately.

Continued

DIRTY

5 large fresh Thai basil or sweet basil leaves

Watermelon, Bergamot Mint + Basil Mini Ice Cubes (page 30) or crushed ice for serving

¼ cup plus 1 Tbsp [75 ml] watermelon + bergamot mint juice (see Note)

3 Tbsp [45 ml] bourbon, such as Buffalo Trace or Old Grand-Dad

2 Tbsp [30 ml] Tomato Consommé (page 60)

1½ Tbsp [22 ml] fresh lemon juice

1 Tbsp [15 ml] Clean or Dirty Basic Simple Syrup (page 69)

½ Tbsp [7.5 ml] rose water (I use Sadaf or Al Wahdi brands; see Resources, page 211)

2 or 3 drops gentian root tincture (see Note, page 161)

Small basil and mint sprigs and/or 1 edible pink rosebud for garnish

Powdered sugar for dusting (optional)

NOTE: *To make 1 cup [240 ml] watermelon + bergamot mint juice, in a blender, combine 1½ cups [225 g] cubed watermelon and ¼ cup [24 g] fresh bergamot mint leaves. Blend until smooth. Alternatively, pass 1½ cups [225 g] cubed watermelon and ¼ cup [24 g] bergamot mint leaves through a juicer. (See the Resources section, page 211, for where to find bergamot mint. If you can't find bergamot mint, substitute regular garden mint.)*

Put the basil leaves in the bottom of a Julep cup or stemless wineglass. Fill the cup with the mini ice cubes or crushed ice. Pour the watermelon + bergamot mint juice, bourbon, consommé, lemon juice, syrup, rose water, and gentian root tincture over the ice. Insert a swizzle stick. Position your palms flat on either side of the swizzle stick and run your hands back and forth to spin and twirl the stick and stir the mixture.

Garnish with the herb sprigs and/or rosebud, dust with powdered sugar, if you like, and serve immediately.

#8

STRAWBERRY + UMEBOSHI + MANZANILLA SHERRY

MAKES 1 CLEAN OR DIRTY COCKTAIL

I'm crazy for anything to do with Japanese food or drink: the culinary sensibility and flavors, the cultural approach to hospitality, and a seemingly innate national ability to improve on anything we Westerners merely dabble in by comparison.

One of my favorite wonders of Japanese culinary traditions is *umeboshi*, the pickled ume fruit common in Japan, often called Japanese pickled plums or Japanese salt plums. The fruits are traditionally pickled in a solution of salt and red shiso, which is a member of the mint family. Shiso, also called perilla, is highly aromatic and often used with raw fish and other pickled vegetables. A by-product of making these salty-sweet pickles is ume plum vinegar, which is great in dressings or drizzled over veggies and fish; both the plums and the vinegar have an alkalizing effect on the stomach, making them a powerful digestive stimulant and detoxification aid, which in turn combats fatigue.

I like to use *umeboshi* plums in place of olives in a Dirty Martini, any clinging vinegar standing in for the olive brine. Another splash of the vinegar contributes to the structure of this drink. You can also find ume paste in most Japanese markets. It is slightly less tart than the vinegar and works better for me in shaken drinks. I reserve the vinegar for stirred cocktails. If you can't find the paste but like the idea of the texture and appearance it would bring to the mix, buy a package of *umeboshi* and pit the plums. Send them through a food processor for your own homemade paste. It pairs beautifully with the strawberries and rose water in this cocktail.

The Clean version of this drink is splendidly refreshing on a hot summer day. Add the nutty, lightly savory, dry sherry for a Spanish twist and *rebujito*-style aperitif quencher.

CLEAN

2 large ripe strawberries, hulled and chopped, plus a slice or two for garnish

¼ cup [60 ml] Strawberry Consommé (page 63)

2 Tbsp [30 ml] ume plum vinegar, or 1 tsp *umeboshi* plum paste (see Resources, page 211)

2 Tbsp [30 ml] fresh lemon juice

1 Tbsp [15 ml] Clean Basic Simple Syrup (page 69)

½ Tbsp [7.5 ml] rose water (I use Sadaf or Al Wahdi brands; see Resources, page 211)

Dash of aquafaba (optional; see page 118)

Ice cubes for shaking and serving

Large mint sprig and a dusting of powdered sugar or pinch of cracked pink peppercorns for garnish

Put the chopped strawberries in the bottom of a tall glass or large wineglass.

In a cocktail shaker, combine the consommé, vinegar, lemon juice, syrup, rose water, and aquafaba (if using). Add 5 ice cubes, cover the shaker, and shake hard for about 3 seconds.

Fill the glass with the strawberries with ice. Using a Hawthorne strainer, strain the drink into the glass. Garnish with the strawberry slices, mint, a dusting of powdered sugar, or the pink peppercorns.

DIRTY

2 large ripe strawberries, hulled and chopped, plus a slice or two for garnish

3 Tbsp [45 ml] Manzanilla sherry

2 Tbsp [30 ml] Strawberry Consommé (page 63)

2 Tbsp [30 ml] ume plum vinegar, or 1 tsp *umeboshi* plum paste (see Resources, page 211)

2 Tbsp [30 ml] fresh lemon juice

2 Tbsp [30 ml] Dirty Basic Simple Syrup (page 69)

½ Tbsp [7.5 ml] rose water (I use Sadaf or Al Wahdi brands; see Resources, page 211)

Dash of aquafaba (optional; see page 118)

Ice cubes for shaking and serving

Large mint sprig and a dusting of powdered sugar or pinch of cracked pink peppercorns for garnish

Put the chopped strawberries in the bottom of a tall glass or large wineglass.

In a cocktail shaker, combine the sherry, consommé, vinegar, lemon juice, syrup, rose water, and aquafaba (if using). Add 5 ice cubes, cover the shaker, and shake hard for about 3 seconds.

Fill the glass with the strawberries with ice. Using a Hawthorne strainer, strain the drink into the glass. Garnish with the strawberry slices, mint, a dusting of powdered sugar, or the pink peppercorns.

9

AVOCADO + CILANTRO + TEQUILA

MAKES 1 CLEAN OR DIRTY COCKTAIL

I like to call this smoothie the Yogi's Choice, named after my two yoga teachers, Yonnus and Courtney, who give us a yogi's choice in class (either restorative or challenging poses), as we feel necessary. Here the choice comes in the form of adding that shot of tequila to make this a kind of holistic potion or keeping it totally Clean. Either way, you will be following your bliss.

For an advanced pose—that is, presentation—of this grounding drink, line the glass with a banana or *hoja santa* (root beer plant) leaf. You can also blend in a scoop of camu camu, matcha, or spirulina powder.

CLEAN

1 ripe avocado, pitted and peeled

¼ cup plus 1 Tbsp [75 ml] fresh pineapple juice

3 Tbsp [45 ml] Clean Falernum Syrup (see Brown Rice Orgeat Variation: Falernum, page 81)

2 Tbsp [30 ml] fresh lime juice

2 Tbsp [30 ml] coconut oil

¼ cup [7 g] chopped fresh cilantro leaves, plus leaves or flowers for garnish

2 or 3 Medjool dates, pitted

1 small jalapeño chile, stemmed and seeded (optional)

1 thin slice grilled pineapple for garnish

In a blender, combine the avocado, pineapple juice, syrup, lime juice, coconut oil, cilantro, dates, and jalapeño (if using). Blend for about 10 seconds on high speed until smooth. Pour into a tall chilled glass. Garnish with the cilantro flowers or leaves and/or the pineapple.

DIRTY

1 ripe avocado, pitted and peeled

3 Tbsp [45 ml] tequila or mezcal

3 Tbsp [45 ml] Clean or Dirty Falernum Syrup (see Brown Rice Orgeat Variation: Falernum, page 81)

2 Tbsp [30 ml] fresh pineapple juice

2 Tbsp [30 ml] fresh lime juice

2 Tbsp [28 g] coconut oil

¼ cup [7 g] chopped fresh cilantro, plus leaves or flowers for garnish

2 or 3 Medjool dates, pitted

1 small jalapeño chile, stemmed and seeded (optional)

1 thin slice grilled pineapple for garnish

In a blender, combine the avocado, tequila, syrup, pineapple juice, lime juice, coconut oil, cilantro, dates, and jalapeño (if using). Blend for about 10 seconds on high speed until smooth.

Pour into a tall chilled glass. Garnish with the cilantro flowers or leaves and/or the pineapple.

NOTE: *For a slushier drink, add some ice to either the Clean or the Dirty version before blending, but I recommend it without (the ice dilutes the flavors).*

#10

<u>LETTUCE</u> + <u>CELERY</u> + <u>MEZCAL</u>

MAKES 1 CLEAN OR DIRTY COCKTAIL

This drink is the closest thing to salad in a glass I have ever made. In case that sounds dull to you, make that a *sexy* salad in a glass. The health-promoting properties of leafy greens are well known—they're packed with fiber, vitamins, and minerals, as well as a powerful anti-inflammatory and anxiety tamers. But lettuce, conversely, has a rich secret history as an aphrodisiac, particularly in ancient Egypt, where it was a common sex symbol—apparently, its relative cos, or romaine lettuce, did much to support the belief with its phallic shape—and was celebrated for its powers of stimulation. Lettuce turns up in Chinese food symbolism as well for fertility, luck, and wealth. And you thought it was just (ahem) a bed for your grilled chicken!

This drink was born from my love of Caesar salad; I even use a Parmesan chip (frico) for garnish—mostly because I want cheese on everything, but I also like the contrasting texture and salty finish it brings. If you're also a cheese-aholic, nibble the chip between each sip for the full experience. The mezcal in the Dirty version has a lovely smoky quality that complements the deep vegetable notes from the celery juice and bitters, and is, in turn, enhanced by the smoked salt. Using the wine-based aperitif also means you need less simple syrup. It adds a lovely fruity note to the drink's finish. If you can't find a sweet white vermouth, such as Dolin Blanc, Martini Bianco works, too, but it has added spice notes that will alter the flavor slightly. See the Resources section (page 211) for where to buy specialty bitters.

CLEAN

3 Tbsp [45 ml] fresh lettuce juice

3 Tbsp [45 ml] fresh celery juice

2 Tbsp [30 ml] fresh lemon juice

2 Tbsp [30 ml] Clean Basic Simple Syrup
(page 69)

¼ tsp ground celery seeds

1 drop alcohol-free gentian root tincture
(see Note, page 161)

Dash of aquafaba (optional; see page 118)

Ice cubes for shaking

1 rock ice cube for serving

Pinch of Maldon smoked sea salt flakes

1 or 2 thin cucumber slices or celery
leaves for garnish

1 Parmesan Frico (page 137) for garnish

In a cocktail shaker, combine the lettuce, celery, and lemon juices, syrup, celery seeds, gentian root tincture, and aquafaba (if using). Add 5 ice cubes, cover the shaker, and shake hard for 3 seconds.

Put the rock ice cube in a rocks or double Old-Fashioned glass. Using a Hawthorne strainer, strain the drink into the glass.

Garnish with a pinch of smoked salt, the cucumber slices or celery leaves, and a Parmesan Frico.

DIRTY

2 Tbsp [30 ml] mezcal

2 Tbsp [30 ml] fortified or aperitif wine,
such as Floc de Gascogne or Cocchi
Americano

1½ Tbsp [22 ml] fresh lettuce juice

1½ Tbsp [22 ml] fresh celery juice

1½ Tbsp [22 ml] fresh lemon juice

1 Tbsp [15 ml] Clean or Dirty Basic Simple
Syrup (page 69)

3 dashes of celery bitters

Dash of aquafaba (optional; see page 118)

Ice cubes for shaking

1 rock ice cube for serving

Pinch of Maldon smoked sea salt flakes

1 or 2 thin cucumber slices or celery
leaves for garnish

1 Parmesan Frico (page 137) for garnish

In a cocktail shaker, combine the mezcal, wine, lettuce, celery, and lemon juices, syrup, bitters, and aquafaba (if using). Add 5 ice cubes, cover the shaker, and shake hard for 3 seconds.

Put the rock cube in a rocks or double Old-Fashioned glass. Using a Hawthorne strainer, strain the drink into the glass.

Garnish with a pinch of smoked salt, the cucumber slices or celery leaves, and a Parmesan Frico.

#11

LEMON VERBENA + VANILLA + GIN

MAKES 1 CLEAN OR DIRTY COCKTAIL

In the sprawling universe of culinary botanicals, another heavenly scent comes from lemon verbena, a perennial shrub with long, glossy, pointed leaves. The intense citrus scent of the leaves is delightful and reviving. I have a small bush growing outside my door, and every morning I sit on the stoop (yes, in my PJs) and inhale its magic. It's a terrific balm against the hectic parts of the day to come.

In my opinion, verbena does not get used nearly enough in modern food and drinks. In addition to its wonderful aromatherapeutic powers, the plant has several medicinal uses—taken in tea or tisanes, it can reduce fever, alleviate stomach problems, and boost your immune system. It's also been shown to help keep muscles healthy. So, next time you reach for that protein powder, think about switching it up with a lovely glass of Lemon Verbena Tisane (page 94) instead.

With its especially delicate and refreshing flavors, this drink is a delicious summery spritz, equally light in a Clean or Dirty version. It's a good recipe for taking out your Perlini shaker, if you have one (see page 15). Otherwise, top it off with a float of bubbles.

CLEAN

Sweet-Tart Powder (page 127) for the rim

1 lemon wedge

¼ cup [60 ml] Lemon Verbena Tisane
(page 94)

2 Tbsp [30 ml] fresh lemon juice

2 Tbsp [30 ml] Clean Basic Simple Syrup
(page 69)

⅛ tsp alcohol-free pure vanilla extract

2 or 3 drops alcohol-free gentian root
tincture (see Note, page 161)

2 Tbsp [30 ml] aquafaba (optional; see
page 118)

Ice cubes for shaking

Tonic or soda water, chilled (optional)

Rim a chilled coupe or Martini glass
with Sweet-Tart Powder: Pour a layer
of powder into a small, shallow dish.
Rub the lemon wedge around the
rim of the glass and dip the rim into
the powder until evenly coated. Tap
gently to remove any loose grains and
set aside.

In a cocktail shaker, combine
the tisane, lemon juice, syrup, vanilla,
gentian root tincture, and aquafaba
(if using). Add 5 ice cubes, cover
the shaker, and shake hard for 5 to
6 seconds.

Using a Hawthorne strainer,
immediately strain the drink into the
prepared glass. Top with a splash of
bubbles, if you like.

DIRTY

Sweet-Tart Powder (page 127) for the rim

1 lemon wedge

¼ cup [60 ml] Lemon Verbena Old Tom
Gin (page 94)

2 Tbsp [30 ml] fresh lemon juice

2 Tbsp [30 ml] Dirty Basic Simple Syrup
(page 69)

2 Tbsp [30 ml] aquafaba (see page 118)
or 1 egg white (optional)

¼ tsp pure vanilla extract

2 or 3 drops gentian root tincture (see
Note, page 161)

Ice cubes for shaking

Prosecco, cava, tonic water, or soda
water, chilled (optional)

Rim a chilled coupe or Martini glass
with Sweet-Tart Powder: Pour a layer
of powder into a small, shallow dish.
Rub the lemon wedge around the
rim of the glass and dip the rim into
the powder until evenly coated. Tap
gently to remove any loose grains and
set aside.

In a cocktail shaker, combine
the gin, lemon juice, syrup, aquafaba
(if using), vanilla, and gentian root
tincture. Add 5 ice cubes, cover
the shaker, and shake hard for 5 to
6 seconds.

Using a Hawthorne strainer,
immediately strain the drink into the
prepared glass. Top with a splash of
bubbles, if you like.

#12

HOLY BASIL + MATCHA GREEN TEA + RUM

MAKES 1 CLEAN OR DIRTY COCKTAIL

Holy basil, or tulsi, is one of those miraculous plants used in Ayurvedic medicine for everything from fighting cancer to treating heart disease, mostly administered in tea form. It's also one of the tastiest herbs out there, bright and pungent with a mildly anise-like flavor, and great in everything from Thai curries to refreshing cold beverages, like this blended drink. Here, a base of either sweetened coconut water or lime-laced rum pairs with another antioxidant wonder, green tea; its bitterness is mellowed in both versions by the fat in a yummy coconut butter–washed simple syrup.

The Dirty recipe here takes its cues from a classic frozen Daiquiri: rum, sugar, and lime juice. The Clean option is a kind of tricked-out limeade, with the green tea supplying a gentle jolt of caffeine.

CLEAN

½ cup [17 g] packed holy basil or Thai basil leaves, plus a small sprig or flower for garnish (see Resources, page 211)

¼ cup plus 2 Tbsp [90 ml] Thai coconut water

3 Tbsp [45 ml] fresh lime juice

3 Tbsp [45 ml] Clean Coconut Butter–Washed Syrup (page 111)

½ tsp matcha green tea powder

2 or 3 drops alcohol-free gentian root tincture (see Note, page 161)

2 cups [240 g] ice or less to taste

In a blender, combine the basil, coconut water, lime juice, syrup, matcha, gentian root tincture, and ice. Blend on high speed for about 10 seconds until smooth. Pour into a large chilled glass. Garnish with the basil sprig or flower.

DIRTY

½ cup [17 g] packed holy basil or Thai basil leaves, plus a small basil sprig or flower for garnish (see Resources, page 211)

¼ cup [60 ml] white rum or coconut rum

3 Tbsp [45 ml] fresh lime juice

3 Tbsp [45 ml] Clean or Dirty Coconut Butter–Washed Syrup (page 111)

½ tsp matcha green tea powder

2 or 3 drops gentian root tincture (see Note, page 161)

2 cups [240 g] ice or less to taste

In a blender, combine the basil, rum, lime juice, syrup, matcha, gentian root tincture, and ice. Blend for about 10 seconds on high speed until smooth. Pour into a large chilled glass. Garnish with the basil sprig or flower.

AUTUMN

This is probably my favorite time of year. Keats's ode "To Autumn" is constantly on my mind, the iambic pentameter of his words perfectly capturing the sensory rhythm of the season—the mists and mellow fruitfulness, the crisp morning air, and the scent of moist soil filling my nostrils and clearing my head. A time to gather and preserve the fleeting bounty from the field and from the market stalls: apples, pears, pomegranates, guavas, and root vegetables.

In fall, my kitchen becomes a fragrant den of shrub and kombucha making, filled with the earthy scents of those rich distillations and fermentations one day and other fruity infusions the next, like my personal Clean and Dirty versions of "Pimm's" (page 95). All these potions are wondrous ways to capture the essences of fall and the seasons that came before, and fill my refrigerator to overflowing, to be joyfully uncorked at a later date for a taste of those peaking days.

In autumn, my usual reliance on fresh garden herbs in the kitchen and on my drink menu shifts to favor hardier herbs and a range of woody, earthy, and nutty aromatics and flavors—dried spices and teas to add underlying tones of warmth and piquancy; grains, such as toasted barley or brown rice, become the best of friends with colder weather's appealing darker spirit choices; and wood-aged whisky and brandies, smoked or vanilla imbued—that offer so many wonderful possibilities for quaffs in fireside repose on rainy nights.

13

GOLDEN BEET + SHISO + SAISON BEER

MAKES 1 CLEAN OR DIRTY COCKTAIL

Please don't judge me, but my very first foray into libatious activity was the simple Shandy. I was about nine years old.

In general, a typical Shandy is half beer and half soft drink, such as lemonade or Sprite or 7UP. In the UK, however, there is a canned version of Shandy called Shandy Bass. It is, indeed, made with "real beer," but the proportion of beer to benign fizz is much less than usual—0.5 percent alcohol, to be exact. So when we were kids, our parents thought nothing of giving us a glassful to keep us quiet while they all got sloshed. In fact, Shandy Bass is still popular with grown-ups for a public daytime tipple.

As the Shandy and I have gotten older, the proportion of beer seems to gradually increase every year—sort of a ritual of passage; it is my favorite refreshment on a Sunday afternoon after working the brutal brunch shift. These days, lovely Shandy variations abound at creative bars, and I was inspired, too, to create this version far from my childhood days, shaped by the earthy flavors of golden beets and shiso leaves. In the delicious Clean version, homemade kombucha inflected with ginger and honey is a drier and tarter substitute for the beer; the apple juice adds a subtle fruitiness.

Continued

CLEAN

¼ cup [60 ml] fresh-pressed apple juice

2 Tbsp [30 ml] Beet + Shiso Shrub (page 113), made with golden beets (see Note)

2 Tbsp [30 ml] Ginger Simple Syrup (page 89)

1 Tbsp [15 ml] fresh lemon juice

2 or 3 drops alcohol-free gentian root tincture (see Note, page 161)

Ice cubes for shaking and serving

2 Tbsp to ¼ cup [30 to 60 ml] Ginger + Manuka Kombucha (page 116)

1 or 2 thin carrot slices for garnish

Edible disco dust for garnish (optional; available from cake decorating supply stores and online)

In a cocktail shaker, combine the apple juice, shrub, syrup, lemon juice, and gentian root tincture. Add 5 ice cubes, cover the shaker, and shake hard for 3 seconds.

Fill a highball glass with ice. Using a Hawthorne strainer, strain the drink into the glass. Top with the kombucha and garnish with the carrot slices. Sprinkle the carrots with disco dust, if you like.

DIRTY

¼ cup [60 ml] fresh-pressed apple juice

2 Tbsp [30 ml] Beet + Shiso Shrub (page 113), made with golden beets (see Note)

2 Tbsp [30 ml] Ginger Simple Syrup (page 89)

1 Tbsp [15 ml] fresh lemon juice

2 or 3 drops gentian root tincture (see Note, page 161)

Ice cubes for shaking

¼ cup [60 ml] saison or pilsner

1 or 2 thin carrot slices for garnish

Edible disco dust for garnish (optional; available from cake decorating supply stores and online)

In a cocktail shaker, combine the apple juice, shrub, syrup, lemon juice, and gentian root tincture. Add 5 ice cubes, cover the shaker, and shake hard for 3 seconds.

Fill a highball glass with ice. Using a Hawthorne strainer, strain the drink into the glass. Top with the beer and garnish with the carrot slices. Sprinkle the carrots with disco dust, if you like.

NOTE: *The golden beet shrub makes a beautiful, sunny Shandy. If you want to get fancy, make it a sunrise (or sunset) by adding a splash of red beet juice to the bottom of the glass before you build the drink for a lovely layered effect. If you want to get really fancy, sprinkle a tiny pinch of disco dust into each layer.*

#14

CARAMEL + APPLE + CALVADOS

MAKES 1 CLEAN OR DIRTY COCKTAIL

I think I'm still in good company when I say autumn is the time of year for caramel apples. In the Motherland, they appear around Guy Fawkes Night in early November; as kids, we would stand in awe of the burning man on the roaring fire, clutching our treats as our faces and hands devolved into a sticky mess.

As a fully fledged adult, I admit that treat has way too much sugar; more than one bite and I'm certain I would sink into a coma. I created this liquid version so I could revel in the nostalgia of my youth without needing a blood transfusion. The caramel syrup is made with miracle ingredients coconut sugar and coconut milk, reducing both calories and refined sugar. A pinch of smoked Maldon sea salt makes it an even more grown-up treat.

CLEAN

¼ cup plus 2 Tbsp [75 ml] fresh-pressed apple juice

2 Tbsp [30 ml] Clean Salted Caramel Syrup (page 82)

2 Tbsp [30 ml] aquafaba (see page 118)

2 Tbsp [30 ml] fresh lemon juice

¼ tsp apple cider vinegar

Ice cubes for shaking

Pinch of Maldon smoked sea salt for garnish

Pinch of freshly grated nutmeg for garnish

Aftelier's Apple Essence for garnish (optional; see Note)

In a cocktail shaker, combine the apple juice, syrup, aquafaba, lemon juice, and vinegar. Add 1 ice cube, cover the shaker, and whip shake for 5 seconds. Add 4 more ice cubes, cover the shaker, and shake hard for 5 seconds more.

Using a Hawthorne strainer, immediately strain the drink into a stemless wineglass. Sprinkle the smoked salt and nutmeg over the surface. Add a spritz of apple essence, if you like.

DIRTY

3 Tbsp [45 ml] Calvados

2 Tbsp [30 ml] fresh-pressed apple juice

2 Tbsp [30 ml] Dirty Salted Caramel
    Syrup (page 82)

2 Tbsp [30 ml] aquafaba (see page 118)
    or 1 egg white

2 Tbsp [30 ml] fresh lemon juice

¼ tsp apple cider vinegar

Ice cubes for shaking

Pinch of Maldon smoked sea salt for
    garnish

Pinch of freshly grated nutmeg for garnish

Aftelier's Apple Essence for garnish
    (optional; see Note)

NOTE: *Aftelier's Apple Essence is a culinary essential oil for atomizing, created by Berkeley-based perfumer Mandy Aftel. She adds these oils into grain alcohol to create a food-grade spritz. The oils can be added in drops to clean drinks or spritzed over dirtier versions. (See Resources, page 211.)*

For extra aroma, garnish with an apple cider geranium leaf, if available. As an alternative, use a fresh sage or bay leaf. Their scents, though different from the geranium, give a more savory note to the drink's bouquet.

In a cocktail shaker, combine the Calvados, apple juice, syrup, aquafaba, lemon juice, and vinegar. Add 1 ice cube, cover the shaker, and whip shake for 5 seconds. Add 4 more ice cubes, cover the shaker, and shake hard for 5 seconds more.

Using a Hawthorne strainer, immediately strain the drink into a stemless wineglass. Sprinkle the smoked salt and nutmeg over the surface. Add a spritz of apple essence, if you like.

15

CARROT + CARDAMOM + APEROL + OLD TOM GIN

MAKES 1 CLEAN OR DIRTY COCKTAIL

Carrots have a vibrant, delicious crunch and flavor when raw, are intoxicatingly sweet when juiced, and are just plain ridiculously good for you. Drinking in all the nutrients and savoriness of the juice is an easy and luxurious way to take in carrots' goodness; for a lighter way to drink their earthy nectar, try the Clean and Dirty cocktails following. The Clean version mixes carrot juice with citrus for a zippy, healthy carrot lemonade; the Dirty version adds dry gin and a splash of Aperol—Italian orange bitters—for a drink that's a perfect fall post-yoga, pre-dinner aperitif, or an evening celebration any time of year.

CLEAN

¼ cup plus 2 Tbsp [90 ml] fresh carrot juice

2 Tbsp [30 ml] Clean Cardamom Simple Syrup (page 69)

1 Tbsp [15 ml] fresh yuzu juice or fresh lime juice

1 Tbsp [15 ml] fresh lemon juice

1 drop alcohol-free gentian root tincture (page 161)

Ice cubes for shaking and serving

Fennel frond, parsley sprig, or pea shoot for garnish

In a cocktail shaker, combine the carrot juice, syrup, yuzu and lemon juices, and gentian root tincture. Add 5 ice cubes, cover the shaker, and shake hard for 3 seconds.

Fill a stemless wineglass or double Old-Fashioned glass with ice cubes. Using a Hawthorne strainer, strain the drink into the glass. Garnish with the fennel frond, parsley sprig, or pea shoot.

DIRTY

3 Tbsp [45 ml] Old Tom gin or other dry gin

3 Tbsp [45 ml] fresh carrot juice

1½ Tbsp [22 ml] Aperol

1 Tbsp [15 ml] fresh yuzu juice or fresh lime juice

1 Tbsp [15 ml] fresh lemon juice

1 Tbsp [15 ml] Dirty Basic Simple Syrup (page 69)

2 dashes of Scrappy's Cardamom Bitters

Ice cubes for shaking

Fennel frond, parsley sprig, or pea shoot for garnish

In a cocktail shaker, combine the gin, carrot juice, Aperol, yuzu and lemon juices, syrup, and cardamom bitters. Add 5 ice cubes, cover the shaker, and shake hard for 3 seconds.

Fill a stemless wineglass or double Old-Fashioned glass with ice cubes. Using a Hawthorne strainer, strain the drink into the glass. Garnish with the fennel frond, parsley sprig, or pea shoot.

#16

BROWN RICE + BANANA + WHITE RUM

MAKES 1 CLEAN OR DIRTY COCKTAIL

Bananas are packed full of vitamins and essential minerals, such as potassium, great for keeping my tired cocktail-shaking muscles cramp free. In both Clean and Dirty recipes, whole-grain brown rice milk and nutrition star cinnamon team up with bananas to make a powerful and tasty superhero duo.

CLEAN

1 ripe but not mushy banana

¼ cup [120 ml] brown rice milk

2 Tbsp [30 ml] Clean Cinnamon Simple Syrup (page 69)

1 Tbsp [15 ml] Brown Butter–Washed Syrup (page 110)

¼ tsp alcohol-free pure vanilla extract

Pinch of Maldon smoked sea salt flakes

Pinch of finely grated orange zest

Crushed ice for serving

Fresh lime leaf for garnish

In a blender, combine the banana, milk, syrups, vanilla, salt, and orange zest. Blend for about 10 seconds on high speed until smooth. Pour into a tall chilled glass and top with crushed ice. With a long-handled mixing spoon, stir 1 or 2 times and garnish with the lime leaf.

DIRTY

¼ cup [60 ml] brown rice milk

3 Tbsp [45 ml] Brown Butter–Washed Banana Rum (page 111)

2 Tbsp [30 ml] Dirty Cinnamon Simple Syrup (page 69)

¼ tsp pure vanilla extract

Pinch of Maldon smoked sea salt flakes

Pinch of finely grated orange zest

Ice cubes for shaking

Crushed ice for serving

Fresh kaffir lime leaf or pineapple frond for garnish

In a cocktail shaker, combine the milk, rum, syrup, vanilla, salt, and orange zest. Add 2 ice cubes and whip shake for 1 to 2 seconds.

Fill a highball glass with crushed ice. Using a Hawthorne strainer, strain the drink into the glass. Garnish with the kaffir lime leaf or pineapple frond.

#17

<u>OOLONG</u> + <u>BLACK LIME</u> + <u>BOURBON</u>

MAKES 1 CLEAN OR DIRTY COCKTAIL

Okay, I'm about to date myself. I grew up in the flare-pants-wearing, platform-shoe-stomping seventies, in a small mining town light-years behind the rest of the modern world in every aspect, except one—the fact that we could buy Coca-Cola in pretty much any corner shop in town. *Have a Coke and a smile . . . It's the Real Thing . . .* I can still hear the jingles in my head, and remember wanting to run away to some far-off hill by the sea where I could join hands with the rest of the world and live in harmony.

But, by my early teens, instead of harmony, I was dealing with cavities galore. Coke was the first casualty on my path to healthier teeth, and all the artificially sweetened colas tasted nothing like the original. Then recently, a taste of that addictive original got me thinking: There had to be a way to make a cola-tasting beverage with better, healthier (non-tooth-rotting!) ingredients. My solution? This versatile syrup concocted with a rad range of spices, all infused in oolong tea for the caffeinated pep as well as the flavor we want in our colas.

The black lime element in this drink also comes from the oolong syrup. Black limes are dried citrus used as a spice in many Middle Eastern preparations.

CLEAN

Crushed ice for serving

¼ cup plus 2 Tbsp [90 ml] Oolong Cola Syrup (page 84)

¼ cup plus 2 Tbsp [90 ml] soda water, chilled (see Note, page 195)

1 Tbsp [15 ml] fresh lime juice

1 drop alcohol-free pure vanilla extract

1 drop alcohol-free gentian root tincture (see Note, page 161)

Pinch of Maldon smoked sea salt flakes (optional)

Lime twist or slice for garnish

Aftelier's Lime Chef's Essence for garnish (optional; see Resources, page 211)

Fill a chilled highball glass with crushed ice. Add the syrup, soda water, lime juice, vanilla, gentian root tincture, and salt (if using). With a long-handled mixing spoon, stir 2 or 3 times.

Squeeze the lime twist over the drink to release the oils and rub it around the rim of the glass, or rub the lime slice around the rim. Drop the peel or slice into the drink. Garnish with a spritz of lime essence, if you like.

Continued

DIRTY

Crushed ice for serving

¼ cup [60 ml] Oolong Cola Syrup (page 84)

¼ cup plus 2 Tbsp [90 ml] soda water, chilled (see Note)

3 Tbsp [45 ml] bourbon, such as Buffalo Trace or Old Grand-Dad, or aged rum

1 Tbsp [15 ml] PX sherry (see Note)

1 Tbsp [15 ml] fresh lime juice

2 dashes of lime bitters

1 drop pure vanilla extract

Pinch of Maldon smoked sea salt flakes (optional)

Lime twist or slice for garnish

Aftelier's Lime Chef's Essence for garnish (optional; see Resources, page 211)

Fill a chilled highball glass with crushed ice. Add the syrup, soda water, bourbon, sherry, lime juice, lime bitters, vanilla, and salt (if using). With a long-handled mixing spoon, stir 2 or 3 times.

Squeeze the lime twist over the drink to release the oils and rub it around the rim of the glass, or run the lime slice around the rim. Drop the peel or slice into the drink. Garnish with a spritz of lime essence, if you like.

NOTE: *Both versions of this drink are suited to a Perlini shaker (see page 15). If you use a Perlini, the soda water and the oolong syrup both need to be very cold so the CO_2 adheres properly to the liquid. CO_2 does not activate very well in warmer mixtures. Build the cocktails as listed, but pour them into the Perlini shaker, add your ice, secure the lid, and charge with CO_2. Shake vigorously for 5 seconds and let the bubbles subside slightly before pouring it into your ice-filled glass.*

PX sherry is used here for a raisin note. It's an aged sherry made from grapes that have been allowed to turn into raisins on the vine, which concentrates both flavor and sugar. (PX sherry is also delicious poured over vanilla ice cream.) The raisin notes pair beautifully with aged spirits, such as bourbon or rum.

#18

POMEGRANATE + HARISSA + SHERRY + MEZCAL

MAKES 1 CLEAN OR DIRTY COCKTAIL

This drink is my homage to the Middle East, featuring an unusual (mixologically speaking) mélange of pomegranate, dates, rose water, harissa, and cumin. (You can find these ingredients at Middle Eastern markets or many well-stocked supermarkets.) Harissa, in case you're not familiar with it, is a paste made from hot chile peppers. The capsaicin that gives them their heat is a powerful anti-inflammatory. It also boosts metabolism and makes your body burn fat faster. Pomegranates, long revered in their native Iran, other parts of the Middle East, and the Mediterranean regions of Asia, Africa, and Europe—and now also in myriad regions and supermarket coolers worldwide—get great marks for nutrition. Among many other benefits, they are high in antioxidants and polyphenols, all good for your skin and blood pressure. On modern-day tables, the fruit is often served with salts and spices as well as aromatic herbs; the juice is slurped on its own and appears in myriad dishes. For these recipes, purchase pure-juice bottled versions (preferably organic); or, if you have the time and patience, juice your own.

For a lower-alcohol version of the Dirty recipe, omit the mezcal and increase the sherry by 1 ounce [30 ml] or so.

CLEAN

¼ cup plus 2 Tbsp [90 ml] pure unsweetened pomegranate juice

2 Tbsp [30 ml] fresh lemon juice

2 Tbsp [30 ml] Date Syrup (page 72)

½ Tbsp [7.5 ml] rose water (I use Sadaf or Al Wahdi brands; see Resources, page 211)

½ tsp harissa

2 drops alcohol-free gentian root tincture (see Note, page 161)

Pinch of ground cumin (optional)

Ice cubes for shaking and serving

Pink peppercorns for garnish

Pomegranate seeds for garnish

In a cocktail shaker, combine the pomegranate juice, lemon juice, syrup, rose water, harissa, gentian root tincture, and cumin (if using). Add 5 ice cubes, cover the shaker, and shake hard for about 3 seconds.

Fill a double Old-Fashioned glass with ice cubes. Using a Hawthorne strainer, strain the drink into the glass. Drop in a pink peppercorn or two and a few pomegranate seeds and serve.

DIRTY

3 Tbsp [45 ml] mezcal

3 Tbsp [45 ml] pure unsweetened
    pomegranate juice

2 Tbsp [30 ml] fresh lemon juice

1 Tbsp [15 ml] Date Syrup (page 72)

1 Tbsp [15 ml] Manzanilla sherry

½ Tbsp [7.5 ml] rose water (I use Sadaf
    or Al Wahdi brands; see Resources,
    page 211)

½ tsp harissa

2 dashes of Peychaud's bitters

Pinch of ground cumin (optional)

Ice cubes for shaking and serving

Pink peppercorns for garnish

Pomegranate seeds for garnish

In a cocktail shaker, combine the mezcal, pomegranate juice, lemon juice, syrup, sherry, rose water, harissa, bitters, and cumin (if using). Add 5 ice cubes, cover the shaker, and shake hard for about 3 seconds.

Fill a double Old-Fashioned glass with ice cubes. Using a Hawthorne strainer, strain the drink into the glass. Drop in a pink peppercorn or two and a few pomegranate seeds and serve.

WINTER

For much of my life, winter was the time for resetting, battening down ye olde hatches, and, generally, hunkering down. While Keats is my poet for autumn, as the cold sets in Dickens's *Great Expectations* and Rossetti's "In the Bleak Midwinter" become my hymnals. Just the thought of these makes me run for my woolies! Then I moved to Los Angeles. Temperatures in La La Land in winter can, of course, be upward of 80°F (26.5°C), even in January—the antithesis of my native UK winters, or New York, for that matter, where the deep-winter chill gets right into your bones and icicles form on your nose hairs.

Drink making can be a bit confusing in winter. Even in Southern California, the farmers' markets are a bit like Mother Hubbard's empty cupboard, with not a whole lot to tinker with. Enter here my own cache of goodies from fall's busy days of putting things by: potions, such as Guava Consommé (page 63), spicy nectars as in Turmeric + Ginger Syrup (page 89), and nutrient-packed basics, such as raw honey and miso, go audaciously into everything from soup to nuts—and I mean *literally*.

Other versatile and tasty pantry items keep things fresh and flavorful—and interesting—at the bar in winter, including seeds and nut milks, tea and honey (especially Manuka), the cranberries that go into perennial action during the holidays, and the transporting spices of tikka masala (see page 78) and chai (see page 76)—all ingredients that suit my goals, as they contain a host of surprising health benefits as well.

#19

GUAVA + CHAI GREEN TEA + BLUE MAJIK + RUM

MAKES 1 CLEAN OR DIRTY COCKTAIL

Most nights that I tend bar, I get the inevitable request (or a half dozen) for "a fruity drink"—and no, not just from so-called girly girls (who by the way, order more whiskey drinks at my bar than the guys do). And often these orders come shyly and under the seeker's breath; the fruity drink is kind of the drink of shame. While these libations are sweet and go down easily, they are a category of cocktail that struggles with being taken seriously. The following represents my efforts to end that.

This fruity mix is made in the style of a tiki drink, which, per-haps, is more whimsical than solemn in its resurgence—but definitely serious about its cocktails. Maybe weirdly, I associate tiki with winter, not summer—likely because I've spent enough winter vacations escap-ing the cold in warmer climates, lapping up many a Banana Daiquiri and Mai Tai by the pool (usually with an imaginary pool boy fanning me with palm fronds). Also, many classic tiki drinks are spicy, accented by cinnamon, allspice, and nutmeg—we Brits don't usually see these flavors until sometime in early December when the indomitable Christmas pudd' arrives, so you can understand my train of thought.

This drink started life as a deconstructed Piña Colada, using pineapple and rum on the bottom and a squirt of whipped coconut cream foam on top. Then I fell in love with guava, and dumped the poor piña portion of the drink. Guava is a powerhouse superfruit, great for skin health, packed full of vitamin C and lycopene (a potent antioxidant), and a proven flu remedy—perfect for boosting your immunity in the colder winter months. A touch of Blue Majik spirulina adds B vitamins and another bunch of minerals to boot. I like to call this beauty the Tiki-Tini. For a festive finish, trick out the coconut foam with a dusting of edible glitter and you'll be thrilled to have this drink in your holiday arsenal.

For a colorful iced chai green tea latte that your local coffee shop will be envious of, forgo the guava and lime juice (and the rum, if making the Dirty recipe), add a shot of coconut milk, shake well, and pour over a tall glass of ice.

Continued

CLEAN

3 Tbsp [45 ml] Guava Consommé
(page 63)

3 Tbsp [45 ml] chai green tea, chilled

2 Tbsp [30 ml] fresh lime juice

1½ Tbsp [22 ml] Coconut Butter–Washed
Syrup (page 111)

2 drops alcohol-free pure vanilla extract

1 drop alcohol-free gentian root tincture
(see Note, page 161)

1 capsule, or about ¼ tsp, Blue Majik
spirulina plus a pinch for garnish
(see Resources, page 211)

Ice cubes for shaking and serving

Coconut-Spiced Foam (page 150)
for garnish

Edible silver glitter for garnish

1 kaffir lime leaf for garnish (see
Resources, page 211)

In a cocktail shaker, combine the consommé, tea, lime juice, syrup, vanilla, gentian root tincture, and spirulina. Add 5 ice cubes, cover the shaker, and shake hard for about 3 seconds.

Fill a Collins glass with ice. Using a Hawthorne strainer, strain the drink into the glass. Top with a shot of coconut foam. Garnish with a pinch of Blue Majik, edible silver glitter, and a kaffir lime leaf placed jauntily on top.

DIRTY

3 Tbsp [45 ml] Guava Consommé
(page 63)

3 Tbsp [45 ml] chai green tea-infused
rum, chilled (see "Infusions,"
page 86, and Note)

2 Tbsp [30 ml] fresh lime juice

1½ Tbsp [22 ml] Coconut Butter–Washed
Syrup (page 111)

2 drops pure vanilla extract

1 drop gentian root tincture
(see Note, page 161)

1 capsule, or about ¼ tsp, Blue Majik
spirulina plus a pinch for garnish
(see Resources, page 211)

Ice cubes for shaking and serving

Coconut-Spiced Foam (page 150)
for garnish

Edible silver glitter for garnish

1 kaffir lime leaf for garnish (see
Resources, page 211)

In a cocktail shaker, combine the consommé, rum, lime juice, syrup, vanilla, gentian root tincture, and spirulina. Add 5 ice cubes, cover the shaker, and shake hard for about 3 seconds.

Fill a Collins glass with ice. Using a Hawthorne strainer, strain the drink into the glass. Top with a shot of coconut foam. Garnish with a pinch of Blue Majik, edible silver glitter, and a kaffir lime leaf placed jauntily on top.

NOTE: *Chai green tea rum is an infusion (see pages 86 to 97) done via sous vide for flash infusion. It can also be a cold infusion, but takes about 24 hours to reach full flavor. To make chai green tea rum, combine 6 chai green tea bags with 4 cups [1 L] rum. See page 67 for sous vide preparation instructions.*

20

BLACK SESAME + DATE + AMARETTO + BOURBON

MAKES 1 CLEAN OR DIRTY COCKTAIL

Amaretto is one of those old-fashioned sweet liqueurs that has been shamed and shunned in recent years for being naff and uncool. However, pair its timeless almond essence with the right cohorts and amaretto comes back into its own as a sophisticated dame of the bar.

In this rich blend, one of those complementary partners is hero ingredient black sesame (see page 43). A dollop of tahini, that beloved silky sesame paste from the Middle East, echoes the nutty flavor of the seeds and adds a blast of health benefits as it's loaded with calcium and B vitamins and works as a bouncer for your liver, helping usher out the toxins hiding in the dark corners.

CLEAN

¾ cup [180 ml] nut milk, such as almond milk or hazelnut milk

6 Medjool dates, pitted

2 Tbsp [30 g] tahini

3 Tbsp [45 ml] Date Syrup (page 72)

1½ tsp black sesame seeds plus a pinch for garnish

¼ tsp alcohol-free bitter almond extract

¼ tsp Maldon smoked sea salt flakes

¼ tsp toasted sesame oil (optional)

Ice cubes or crushed ice for blending

1 dried orange slice (page 143) for garnish

Date Fluid Gel (page 121) for garnish

In a blender, combine the nut milk, dates, tahini, syrup, black sesame seeds, bitter almond extract, salt, sesame oil (if using), and 1 generous scoop of ice [about 1 cup, or 140 g]. Pulse 3 or 4 times to break up the ice and blend for about 15 seconds on high speed until smooth. Pour into a chilled wineglass. Garnish with black sesame seeds, the orange slice, and a dollop of date fluid gel.

DIRTY

¼ cup plus 2 Tbsp [90 ml] nut milk, such
   as almond milk or hazelnut milk

¼ cup [60 ml] bourbon, such as Buffalo
   Trace or Old Grand-Dad

2 Tbsp [30 ml] amaretto

6 Medjool dates, pitted

2 Tbsp [30 g] tahini

3 Tbsp [45 ml] Date Syrup (page 72)

1½ tsp black sesame seeds plus a pinch
   for garnish

¼ tsp Maldon smoked sea salt flakes

¼ tsp toasted sesame oil (optional)

Ice cubes or crushed ice for blending

1 dried orange slice (page 143) for
   garnish

Amaretto Fluid Gel (page 121) for garnish

In a blender, combine the nut milk, bourbon, amaretto, dates, tahini, syrup, black sesame seeds, salt, sesame oil (if using), and 1 generous scoop of ice [about 1 cup, or 140 g]. Pulse 3 or 4 times to break up the ice and blend for about 15 seconds on high speed until smooth. Pour into a chilled wineglass. Garnish with black sesame seeds, the orange slice, and a dollop of amaretto fluid gel.

#21

CHAMOMILE + BEE POLLEN + RIESLING OR HIGHLAND WHISKY

MAKES 1 CLEAN OR DIRTY COCKTAIL

When I formulate recipes, free association guides me—or maybe "focused association" is a better way of putting it. This drink is a good example, as it combines essences of summer with the winter pantry. I begin by focusing on a hero ingredient (see page 43), here chamomile. That ingredient plants a seed and I let the story grow from there, either down to its roots or up to its branches. Maybe that's just following nature . . .

This recipe began with soothing, meadow-scented chamomile, which led me to think about the bees that pollinate this herb, which then led me to bee pollen—a magical manna of spring and summer. This delicate powder from the center of flowers contains the food for everything a hardworking bee needs to grow into a fully fledged buzzing machine: 40 percent protein and packed with amino acids, vitamins, and minerals. On top of all that nutrition, bee pollen is a very effective antibacterial and antifungal for reducing inflammation in our human bodies.

In the transition from free-focused association to tested libation, I found that chamomile, bee pollen, and a honey syrup infused with cardamom, a flowery-flavored spice, pair beautifully—creating a heady, soothing bouquet. When I experimented with adding booze to the mix, a Highland Scotch whisky heightened the aromatics further still, coaxing out strong notes of heather or ripe fruit. By then I knew that fresh citrus juice would be just the thing to cut the sweetness and I was done.

For a lower-ABV version of this drink, a bright herbal white wine, such as a dry Riesling, works really well in place of the whisky. And to connect summer and winter in yet another truly sublime way, gently warm either version over low heat for an aromatic, soothing hot toddy. Buy bee pollen at your local health food store and look for pollen from local bees—it will help with seasonal allergies, or so say the homeopaths who believe that small doses of the offending allergen actually mitigate its effects.

CLEAN

¼ cup plus 1 Tbsp [75 ml] Chamomile Tisane (see "Teas + Tisanes," page 103)

2 Tbsp [30 ml] Clean Spice-Infused Raw Honey Syrup (infused with cardamom; page 70)

2 Tbsp [30 ml] aquafaba (see page 118)

1 Tbsp [15 ml] fresh yuzu juice or fresh lime juice

1 Tbsp [15 ml] fresh lemon juice

2 or 3 drops alcohol-free gentian root tincture (see Note, page 161)

Rock ice cubes for shaking and serving

Bee pollen for garnish (see Resources, page 211)

In a cocktail shaker, combine the tisane, syrup, aquafaba, yuzu and lemon juices, and gentian root tincture. Add 5 ice cubes, cover the shaker, and shake hard for 3 seconds.

Fill a double Old-Fashioned glass with 1 rock ice cube. Using a Hawthorne strainer, immediately strain the drink into the glass. Garnish with a tiny pinch of bee pollen—it's very potent in flavor and aroma and can bully out other flavors if not used sparingly.

DIRTY

3 Tbsp [45 ml] Scotch whisky or dry Riesling wine

2 Tbsp [30 ml] Chamomile Vermouth (page 91)

2 Tbsp [30 ml] Raw Honey Syrup (page 70)

2 Tbsp [30 ml] aquafaba (see page 118) or 1 egg white

1 Tbsp [15 ml] fresh yuzu juice or fresh lime juice

1 Tbsp [15 ml] fresh lemon juice

2 dashes of cardamom bitters

Rock ice cubes for shaking and serving

Bee pollen for garnish (see Resources, page 211)

In a cocktail shaker, combine the whisky, vermouth, syrup, aquafaba, yuzu and lemon juices, and cardamom bitters. Add 5 ice cubes, cover the shaker, and shake hard for 3 seconds.

Fill a double Old-Fashioned glass with 1 rock ice cube. Using a Hawthorne strainer, immediately strain the drink into the glass. Garnish with a tiny pinch of bee pollen—it's very potent in flavor and aroma and can bully out other flavors if not used sparingly.

#22

CRANBERRY + FALERNUM + APPLE CIDER + CALVADOS

MAKES 1 CLEAN OR DIRTY COCKTAIL

The Cape Codder is a fancy name for the rather plain perennial favorite cranberry and vodka cocktail. But cranberries deserve to be much more desirable, and even crave-able, than that jolly-holiday bit of red on an otherwise drab brown plate. Talk about packing an antioxidant punch: Cranberries are in the cancer-fighting hero league. On top of that, these badass berries are high in vitamin C. Surely it's a cranberry (or five) a day that keeps the doctor away!

CLEAN

3 Tbsp [45 ml] Falernum Syrup (see Brown Rice Orgeat Variation: Falernum, page 81)

3 Tbsp [45 ml] fresh lime juice

2 Tbsp [30 ml] pure unsweetened cranberry juice

1 Tbsp [15 ml] aquafaba (see page 118)

5 fresh or frozen cranberries

¼ tsp orange flower water

2 drops alcohol-free gentian root tincture (see Note, page 161)

Ice cubes for shaking and serving

Sparkling apple cider, chilled

In a cocktail shaker, combine the syrup, lime juice, cranberry juice, aquafaba, cranberries, orange flower water, and gentian root tincture. Add 5 ice cubes, cover the shaker, and shake hard for about 3 seconds.

Pour the shaker contents into a Collins glass or large wineglass. Add more ice if desired. Top with sparkling cider.

DIRTY

3 Tbsp [45 ml] Calvados

2 Tbsp [30 ml] Falernum Syrup (see Brown Rice Orgeat Variation: Falernum, page 81)

2 Tbsp [30 ml] fresh lime juice

1 Tbsp [15 ml] Clear Creek cranberry liqueur

1 Tbsp [15 ml] aquafaba (see page 118)

5 fresh or frozen cranberries

¼ tsp orange flower water

2 drops gentian root tincture (see Note, page 161)

Sparkling dry hard cider, chilled

In a cocktail shaker, combine the Calvados, syrup, lime juice, cranberry liqueur, aquafaba, cranberries, orange flower water, and gentian root tincture. Add 5 ice cubes, cover the shaker, and shake hard for about 3 seconds.

Pour the shaker contents into a Collins glass or large wineglass. Add more ice if desired. Top with hard cider.

TURMERIC + TIKKA MASALA + VODKA

MAKES 1 CLEAN OR DIRTY COCKTAIL

I call this one the Mumbai Mule because it's inspired by the classic gingery Moscow Mule. I use ginger and turmeric for flavor and tikka masala spices for depth and warmth. The benefits of turmeric are plentiful—most importantly it's a powerful anti-inflammatory. Keep turmeric in your arsenal of pain relievers. The fresh root is by far the most potent source of goodness—but, in a pinch, use a good-quality powder.

CLEAN

1½ Tbsp [22 ml] Turmeric + Ginger Syrup (page 89)

1½ Tbsp [22 ml] Tikka Masala Syrup (page 78)

3 Tbsp [45 ml] Thai coconut milk

2 Tbsp [30 ml] fresh lime juice

Ice cubes for shaking

Rock ice cubes for serving

Aftelier's Galangal Chef's Essence for garnish (optional; see Resources, page 211)

Curry leaf, edible marigold, or small cilantro sprig for garnish (optional)

In a cocktail shaker, combine the syrups, coconut milk, and lime juice. Add 5 ice cubes, cover the shaker, and shake hard for about 3 seconds.

Fill a chilled stemless wineglass or double Old-Fashioned glass with rock ice. Using a Hawthorne strainer, strain the drink into the prepared glass. Spritz with the galangal essence (if using) and garnish with a curry leaf, marigold, or cilantro sprig (if using).

DIRTY

¼ cup [60 ml] Turmeric + Ginger Vodka (page 89)

2 Tbsp [30 ml] Tikka Masala Syrup (page 78)

2 Tbsp [30 ml] Thai coconut milk

2 Tbsp [30 ml] fresh lime juice

Ice cubes for shaking

Rock ice cubes for serving

Aftelier's Galangal Chef's Essence for garnish (optional; see Resources, page 211)

Curry leaf, edible marigold, or small cilantro sprig for garnish (optional)

In a cocktail shaker, combine the vodka, syrup, coconut milk, and lime juice. Add 5 ice cubes, cover the shaker, and shake hard for about 3 seconds.

Fill a chilled stemless wineglass or double Old-Fashioned glass with rock ice. Using a Hawthorne strainer, strain the drink into the prepared glass. Spritz with the galangal essence (if using) and garnish with a curry leaf, marigold, or cilantro sprig (if using).

MISO + MANUKA HONEY + ISLAY WHISKY

MAKES 1 CLEAN OR DIRTY COCKTAIL

One of my favorite wintertime treats is a hot cup of miso soup laced with a splash (or two, or three) of smoky, briny Islay whisky. Miso, made from fermented soybean paste, contains a plethora of amino acids, enzymes, and microorganisms that help keep our bodies healthy. Plain and simple miso soup is a very effective tool for detoxifying— winter or anytime. And while its flavor is decidedly salty, I think it also displays assertive sweet and umami characteristics, making miso a great ingredient for combining in creative ways.

Islay whisky is produced on an island off the coast of Scotland, and is therefore a true Scotch. I have a fondness for this spirit, as it was my Pops Iggy's favorite tipple. To this day, when I smell Islay whisky, it conjures up an image of my dad rubbing his hands together and looking like the cat that got the cream as he poured his nightly portion.

CLEAN

¼ cup plus 1 Tbsp [75 ml] fresh-brewed roasted barley tea

3 Tbsp [45 ml] Miso–Manuka Honey Syrup (page 70)

2 Tbsp [30 ml] fresh lemon juice

½ tsp ground ginger

¼ tsp cayenne pepper

2 drops alcohol-free pure vanilla extract

1 drop alcohol-free gentian root tincture (see Note, page 161)

1 slice of lemon for garnish

3 or 4 whole cloves for garnish

In a heavy-bottomed saucepan over medium-low heat, combine the tea, syrup, lemon juice, ginger, cayenne, vanilla, and gentian root tincture. Warm through, stirring to dissolve the honey, but do not let boil. Pour into a warmed mug and garnish with lemon and cloves.

DIRTY

¼ cup [60 ml] Islay whisky

3 Tbsp [45 ml] Miso–Manuka Honey Syrup (page 70)

2 Tbsp [30 ml] fresh lemon juice

½ tsp ground ginger

¼ tsp cayenne pepper

2 drops pure vanilla extract

1 drop gentian root tincture (see Note, page 161)

1 slice of lemon for garnish

3 or 4 whole cloves for garnish

In a heavy-bottomed saucepan over medium-low heat, combine the whisky, syrup, lemon juice, ginger, cayenne, vanilla, and gentian root tincture. Warm through, stirring to dissolve the honey, but do not let boil. Pour into a warmed mug and garnish with lemon and cloves.

RESOURCES

LOCAL (SOUTHERN CALIFORNIA) FARMERS
(without websites, but please look out for them at the Santa Monica Farmers' Market if you happen to be visiting)
Coleman Family Farms
Garcia Farms
Schaner Family Farms

AFTELIER
www.aftelier.com
Botanical essences, perfumes, and Chef's Essences

BAR KEEPER
www.barkeepersilverlake.com
Vintage barware, glassware, artisan bitters, and hard-to-find spirits

CHUBO KNIVES
www.chuboknives.com
Japanese barware (jiggers, mixing spoons, glasses), kitchen knives

COCKTAIL KINGDOM
www.cocktailkingdom.com
Cocktail tools, bitters, books, glassware, and mule mugs

DANDELION BOTANICAL COMPANY
www.dandelionbotanical.com
Bulk herbs, spices, essential oils, reishi tincture, and other homeopathic botanicals

DRAGON HERBS
www.dragonherbs.com
Chinese tonic herbs and superfoods, reishi tincture

E3 LIVE
www.e3live.com
Blue Majik spirulina

GOURMET FOOD WORLD
www.gourmetfoodworld.com
Flower waters, edible glitter, vinegars, verjus, culinary oils

GOURMET SWEET BOTANICALS
www.gourmetsweetbotanicals.com
Edible flowers (marigolds, nasturtium), pea tendrils, flowering mint, and fennel

HASHEMS
www.hashems.com
Middle Eastern pantry staples, black limes, dried spices, orange flower water, and rose water

ISI
www.isi.com
Culinary whippers and soda syphons

KALUSTYAN'S
www.kalustyans.com
Specialty market in New York City known for Indian and Middle Eastern spices, such as bitter orange peel, teas, and other global food items; also verjus, pomegranate molasses, vinegars, and gourmet salts

KOMBUCHA KAMP
www.kombuchakamp.com
Scoby

LABEL PEELERS
www.labelpeelers.com
Bitter orange peel

MITSUWA MARKETPLACE
www.mitsuwa.com
Japanese produce, such as teas, yuzu, kaffir lime leaves, umeboshi plum paste, ume plum vinegar, shiso, turmeric, and galangal. Stores are mostly on the West Coast; check the Internet for store locales and online shopping.

MODERNIST PANTRY

www.modernistpantry.com
Modernist pantry ingredients, such as agar, lecithin, and sucro; tools, including immersion circulators, spherification syringes, and whippers

MOON JUICE

moonjuice.com
Bee pollen, plant-based vitality dusts, supplements, and tonics

MOUNTAIN ROSE HERBS

www.mountainroseherbs.com
Flower waters and hydrosols

PERLAGE

www.perlagesystems-accessories.com
Perlini cocktail shaker system

POLYSCIENCE

polyscienceculinary.com
Immersion circulators, cold-smokers, vacuum-sealers, and flash-freezers

SUGAR AND SPUN

www.sugarandspun.com
Organic cotton candy in creative flavors

THE MIXING GLASS

the-mixing-glass.shoplightspeed.com
Vintage glassware, extensive range of cocktail bitters, and unusual spirits

SUR LA TABLE

www.surlatable.com
Edible silver glitter

WINDROSE FARM

www.windrosefarm.org
Rose geranium, bergamot mint, Thai basil, holy basil, red-veined crab apples, fennel flowers, lemon verbena

FURTHER READING

WEBSITES

Cooking Issues: *www.cookingissues.com*

Cook's Science: *www.cooksscience.com*

Gather Journal: *gatherjournal.com*

The Loving Cup: *www.lalovingcup.com*

BOOKS

Crum, Hannah. *The Big Book of Kombucha: Brewing, Flavoring, and Enjoying the Health Benefits of Fermented Tea.* North Adams, MA: Storey Publishing LLC, 2016.

Liu, Kevin K. *Craft Cocktails at Home: Offbeat Techniques, Contemporary Crowd-Pleasers, and Classics Hacked with Science.* Self-published, Amazon Digital Services, 2013.

Morgenthaler, Jeffrey. *The Bar Book: Elements of Cocktail Technique.* San Francisco: Chronicle Books, 2014.

Tosi, Christina. *Momofuku Milk Bar.* New York: Clarkson Potter, 2011.

INDEX

213

ACKNOWLEDGMENTS

Clean+Dirty Drinking would not be possible without the following people:

Thank you with all my heart to Joy Limanon for connecting the dots, and to her crew of dedicated angels; to Patrick O'Brien Smith for dealing with my meltdowns with humor and patience; and to Nicole Tourtelot for always pushing for the best.

To Elaine Breiger and Koppel Kandelzucker for teaching me composition and editing; Lynette Marrero, Jim Kearns, and Michael Voltaggio for lighting the initial spark; and my cheerleading squad, Sam, Kyle, Aaron, Corvette, Sara, Jessica, Lena, and Caroline, for keeping that flame from going out. To perfectionist farmers Barbara Spencer, Romeo Coleman, Peter Schaner, and Lety Garcia for growing the best of everything, and to Geri Miller at The Cooks Garden for the on the fly conjuring up of stunning botanicals for this book.

A special thank you to Chefs Brendan Collins and David Kuo for letting my creative freak flag fly without question or doubt, and to the team of talented bartenders that I get to work with every day. Thank you for supporting me on this journey. A huge thank you to Maggie and Grant for saying my favorite word, "yes," and to my editor, Sarah, for your guidance.

Lastly, I would like to say thank you to my family for putting up with this black sheep and not selling me to the gypsies. *Ile swiat na niebie tyle mam serce dla ciebie!*

Sending you all endless Love + Light!